CUSTOM DESIGN YOUR
OWN DESTINY

Published by
Bruce Goldberg, Inc.
4300 Natoma Ave.
Woodland Hills, CA 91364
Telephone: (800) KARMA-4-U or
FAX: (818) 704-9189
Email: drbg@sbcglobal.net
Web Site:
www.drbrucegoldberg.com

Printed in the United States of America

ISBN 1-57968-014-3

CUSTOM DESIGN YOUR OWN DESTINY

Dr. Bruce Goldberg

Dedication

This book is dedicated to my patients who were open and generous enough to relate their breakthroughs as a result of applying the hypnotic techniques I trained them to utilize. In addition, I dedicate this book to my loyal readers, without whose support this new book would not have been possible.

Note to the Reader

This book is the result of the professional experiences accumulated by the author since 1974, working individually with over 11,000 patients. The material included is intended to complement, not replace, the advice of your own physician, psychotherapist or other health care professional, whom you should always consult about your circumstances prior to starting or stopping any medication or any other course of treatment, exercise regimen or diet.

At times the masculine pronoun has been used as a convention. It is intended to imply both male and female genders where this is applicable. All names and identifying references, except those of celebrities, have been altered to protect the privacy of my patients.

All other facts are accurate and have not been altered.

Dr. Bruce Goldberg

Foreword

As only he could do, the inimitable Dr. Bruce Goldberg has taken the concept of 'self-help' and vaulted it into the new millennium. Is your personal future changeable? Can you actually program your destiny? "Yes," says Dr. Goldberg, emphatically. Citing quantum physics and numerous fascinating case histories, Dr. Goldberg now gives a new incarnation to old cliche 'the power of positive thinking.'

As always, the reader is in store for a rollicking and highly informative good time with this book, which provides all the surprisingly easy tools and techniques necessary to help the reader take control of his/her life and achieve new levels of success. This book is indispensable for those who are tired of having life kick them in the seat of the pants; it is also a marvelous read for people in the business of helping people. Great Goldberg. . .wonderful reading!

- Jeff Rense, Host, The Jeff Rense Radio Show

Table Of Contents

Introduction

The basic theme of this book is that the future is mutable; it is not fixed. By using time-tested and simple techniques, people can literally program their future. I refer to this as custom designing one's destiny. We will deal with consciousness expansion (chapter 14) and removing "self-defeating sequences," actions of self-sabotage, in chapters 3 and 4 in order to train you how to become a more empowered person. It is only by removing the "baggage" that has kept you from achieving certain goals that you can create your own reality.

Quantum physics demonstrates that if we aren't in a certain state of consciousness, certain things cannot be perceived. This requires an expansion and development of our consciousness in order to create the kind of world we desire.

Are you looking for ways to improve your life? This book's purpose is to present an easy-to-use, natural method for succeeding in any endeavor. The material presented is a most unique approach that I have been developing since 1974 and successfully utilize myself (see chapter 1). It doesn't really matter what your personal definition or motives for success are. These may be entirely personal, professional or a combination of both. You will learn how to do a step-by-step access to your higher levels of consciousness and actually perceive your future options. Notice I state future options and not just one future. This concept is fully developed in chapter 12. Specific methods will be given to you to lie out these options. Select the ideal one and literally program yourself for your most desirable reality. You cannot successfully apply these techniques by merely passively reading about them. You must actively engage in these exercises and acquire the background presented to construct and integrate your own personal blueprint for success.

There are unique approaches I will present such as how to design your future (chapter 11) and the "New-You" technique (chapter 12). Beliefs are definitely a major factor in your potential for success, and we will thoroughly instruct you how to contour your beliefs to attain goals. (See chapters 3, 5 and 6). Visualization techniques will be presented throughout this book, in addition to self-hypnosis exercises. You will learn how to overcome fear (chapter 7), get control of your life (chapter 9), become more assertive (chapter 13) and expand your consciousness (chapter 14).

Remember, if you can't do something about your problem, it's not a problem; it's a fact of life. The pessimist complains about the wind. The optimist expects it to change. You, as an empowered soul, will learn how to adjust the sails.

This book will be particularly relevant to you if you answer "No" to any of the following questions:

- Can you avoid the tendency to complain?
- Are you able to avoid worry about the future?
- Do you welcome the unknown?
- Have you eliminated procrastination as a lifestyle?

- Are you treated by others the way you want to be?
- Are you a doer rather than a critic?
- Have you eliminated all blame and fault finding from your life?
- Are you motivated from within rather than from without?
- Are you motivated by your potential for growth, rather than by a need to repair your deficiencies?
- Have you eliminated all dependency relationships?
- Are you free from the need for approval?
- Are you free from ever feeling guilty?
- Have you attained the most important goals of your life?
- Do you custom design your own destiny in a fully empowered and fulfilling way?

If you are interested in eliminating self-defeating sequences that have acted as obstacles to your success and fulfillment, then read on. If you would like to increase your motivation, make more money in less time, reduce financial and other stresses, obtain any job you desire, attract higher quality people into your life, create abundance and become enlightened spiritually, then this book is for you.

By becoming psychically empowered, you will learn to take charge of your life and experience a future of adventure and challenge, rather than one of maintenance and boredom. You, and not the world around you, will establish goals and make them happen. Previous victimization and other dysfunctional patterns will be removed from your awareness.

Read on and introduce yourself to a world beyond your wildest dreams. See the light at the end of the tunnel and master life changing methods that benefit both you and the universe. Here are just some of the methods you will acquire by practicing the many exercises presented in this book.

Learn how to be more creative and productive.

Discover how to bring spirituality into your life and effect win-win-win situations.

Experience both professional and personal rejuvenation.

Become more empowered and successful, and generate these effects to others.

Regain control over your soul's direction and purpose.

Learn techniques of self-hypnosis to program your subconscious mind to make dynamic changes in your being and attract abundance.

We, each as individuals, are the makers of our own destiny, the captains of our ship and the masters of our fate. Our choice is to improve or lower the quality of our destiny by the decisions we make and the actions we take.

This book is about integration. It brings you back to the basics of establishing spirituality and a life purpose characterized by values and ethics. From this foundation, empowerment and abundance techniques are taught. Be prepared for the experience of a lifetime.

By being solely responsible for our blueprint for our future, there are no acceptable excuses for what happens. We are more apt to recognize these excuses in the lives of others than in our own. We are occasionally conscious of the direction and possible future toward which the massed thought of humanity is driving. We do this by bringing into play certain subtle faculties we all possess. This book is designed to teach you how to understand and develop these faculties to the degree that you, yourself, may custom design your own destiny.

Dr. Bruce Goldberg

Chapter 1
Custom Designing A Movie

Before I begin to cover the basics of taking charge of your life (both personal and professional empowerment) and actually custom designing your own future, a personal example of the successful application of these principles and techniques is in order. In the world we live in, talk is cheap. My experience with human nature long ago convinced me that individuals want to see someone 'walk the walk' and practice what they preach. The example I am about to present encompasses many principles of empowerment, consciousness raising and the custom designing of a reality that is the basis of this book.

On Christmas day in 1990 I decided to do a little global assessment of my professional life. Earlier that year I had the pleasure of being interviewed on the *Joan Rivers* Show in New York. My query to my higher self dealt with the question of how to get the message out concerning personal empowerment through self-hypnosis. The only book I had written at that time, *Past Lives—Future Lives*, was the main emissary for my message. Please don't misunderstand my comments about talk shows (i.e., the *Joan Rivers* example). I love doing them and am available whenever a producer calls my Los Angeles office. I just felt that other options were out in the universe and decided to utilize the techniques presented in this book to accomplish this professional goal. Well-meaning friends and colleagues suggested I do infomercials or buy ads in various publications, and on radio and television.

Something inside me just flatly rejected those ideas as being against my style. Upon initiating my own 'custom design your future' technique (see chapter 11), I came up with the idea of having one of my cases aired in a movie for television. At this time I should tell you that although my hypnotherapy practice is located in Los Angeles, I didn't have any contacts to successfully negotiate such a deal. Yes, my patient list includes producers, writers, actors and television and studio executives, but the delicate mechanism to consummate a television movie project just wasn't there. My policy is not to solicit my patients for my own professional advancement.

My lack of experience in such matters also left me in a quandary. It is not my modus operandi to simply make dozens of telephone calls in an attempt to pitch a movie project to the networks. The best way to become a part of such a project is to somehow get the interest of a well-connected executive producer with a proven track record with the networks. I had no such contact.

While continuing my daily programming for this goal, I simply went on with my life. Timing is a critical factor in any custom designing approach. No matter how motivated and excited you may be about a particular project, sometimes you just have to be patient and wait for other factors to line up.

Approximately four months later I was interviewed by a local Los Angeles talk radio station (KFI) on the Joe Crummey Show. Prior to this interview, I had regressed two of Joe's listeners into their past lives. They discussed their experiences with myself, Joe, and the listeners who called in during this live talk show.

As a media consultant and experienced guest on radio and television shows since 1980, this was hardly a unique experience for me. The significance of that interview manifested itself a few days later. A man named Tom called me concerning my interview. He was a television producer and wanted to discuss the possibility of doing a television movie with one of my cases.

This represented the first link in the chain. I naturally expressed interest and asked him what type of case he was looking for. Having conducted over 33,000 past-life regressions on over 11,000 individual patients since 1974, there was quite a spectrum to search.

Tom's requirements were quite specific. He wanted a case featuring a woman in some sort of danger, and it had to be documented. I quickly learned that television movies are targeted for a female audience. That was no problem since over eighty-five percent of my patients are women. The problem was documentation. I do not fly around the world documenting what my patients tell me in trance. Even if I could verify such intimate details from a previous life, my reading of the public is that it would not significantly alter their views on the subject of reincarnation. Besides, there are plenty of documented cases in the literature.

My thoughts immediately were drawn to a female patient named Ivy, whose case I had completed just three years before. This patient was obsessed with a married man she was dating. Johnny was a physically and psychologically abusive businessman, and Ivy just couldn't resist him. He had beat Ivy and literally tried to kill her on two occasions. There was a third attempt on her life during the course of Ivy's hypnotherapy. This was a karmic relationship characterized by the fact that Johnny actually murdered Ivy 20 times in their 46 lives together! A better case for this pending television movie couldn't possibly exist.

There were two initial factors that had to be set up. First, the patient (Ivy) had to assign the rights to this case over to me so I could negotiate with the producer and/or network. Second, this case had to be documented.

The first consideration was not a problem since Ivy had signed a release giving me the right to represent her case in all media any way I chose. A quick check of my chart revealed a simple solution to the second factor - documentation. Over the years I have hired college students to research certain cases for the purpose of documentation. At the end of July in 1988, I contacted one of my researchers in reference to another project. She informed me that she was just about to go to Toronto for a month and would be unavailable until September.

Ivy's last life ended in Buffalo, New York, in May of 1927. Her name was Grace Doze in that incarnation. Geographically Toronto is located just on the other side of Niagara Falls from Buffalo. The universe had provided me with a very practical solution to this documentation problem. My researcher agreed to stop off in Buffalo on her way to Toronto. When she returned I was informed that on May 17, 1927, a Grace Doze had been murdered in Buffalo. The murder was never solved.

This was to my advantage. The only problem was that when I asked my researcher for a copy of the newspaper article, I found that she had neglected to obtain one when she was in the Buffalo library. She did inform me that the murder was reported in the *Buffalo Evening News* on May 21, 1927. I attached this note to Ivy's chart. Now all that was required was a telephone call to the *Buffalo Evening News* to request a copy of that article. The Buffalo newspaper secretary was most helpful and immediately forwarded me a copy of said article.

Later I was to find out that there were several articles written on this case in four Buffalo newspapers. This initial article revealed that not only did a Grace Doze exist, but also that she died exactly as Ivy had described. This article corroborated several other facts related to me by Ivy.

The next step was to set up a meeting with the producer and his partner. In Los Angeles you don't just go to a meeting, you "do breakfast" or "do lunch," and so on. Well, I did breakfast in Bel Air with the producer and met his partner.

I actually liked Tom's partner better than I liked Tom, because meeting Tom in person left me with the uneasy feeling that I simply could not trust him. Subsequent attempts by Tom to get me to sign on the dotted line with his one-way option agreement only buttressed my low opinion of him.

Then in early June, a most fortuitous event happened. One of my East Coast, writer friends had relocated to Los Angeles and contacted me about doing a television movie. This was most interesting timing - synchronistic to say the least.

Alex had proposed various projects to me prior to this call, but none had become a reality. My advice to Alex was to attach an executive producer to his idea and call me back. I did forward him a summary of the Grace Doze case with a copy of the Buffalo article.

Since I hadn't signed any agreement and I owned the rights to Ivy's case, it was quite permissible for me to negotiate with as many prospective buyers as possible. That procedure is the norm in Hollywood, as well as in publishing and most other businesses.

Admittedly, I didn't feel Alex would be able to bring in an executive producer so quickly as to limit my focus on his proposal. Fortunately, I was incorrect and Alex came through with an "A-list" producer. It was a simple matter to meet with the executive producer and Alex and close the deal. Tom was informed of the removal of this project from the open market, and I wished him good luck in his future endeavors.

The next hurdle to surpass was getting a network to buy the project. Since this meeting with the producer, Alex and myself took place in September 1991, I knew that the network would be pitched within a month or so. I was now "out of the loop" until a network showed interest. My life went on as usual, except that another synchronistic event was to play itself out. It should be pointed out at this time that a lot of factors were involved in my meeting Alex back in 1984. The details of these synchronicities, as well as the very dynamic case of Grace Doze and several others of Ivy's past lives, can be found in my book, *The Search for Grace.*

September is when most of the new talk shows premier. Although they can appear at any time of the year, the fall is when the majority of these media forums debut. Some talk shows initially air as a test market show, appearing in only a few markets to fine-tune them for a national exposure. The *Montel Williams Show* was one of them.

When they called me for a pre-interview I decided to do it. This show was originally taped in CBS's Television City in Hollywood. This meant I did not have to fly across country for this test market show. My pre-interview was held on a Friday afternoon in late September. During this time I regressed one of the show's researchers, Mary, to demonstrate the technique of past-life regression hypnotherapy.

Mary (age 25) regressed to a life during the 1940s in which she was being interrogated by a group of men concerning the location of a male fugitive friend of hers. At the end of this regression I guided Mary to the superconscious mind level where she felt "suspended in air" and completely at peace with the universe.

When Montel was informed about this experience, he challenged me to regress him in his private office. I accepted this challenge and regressed Montel with his brother Herman as a witness. Montel's former life was as a slave in the south during the Civil War. Several white farmers beat him to death. This was a very emotional experience for the usually unemotional and matter-of-fact Montel. He stated on the air, "I felt very, very nervous and very, very scared." Needless to say, Montel approved of my appearance on his show.

My interview was scheduled for taping on October 14th. I spent the weekend calling some of my patients to ask them if they would discuss their experiences on the air. One couple perfect for the show agreed but would not be available until October 10 since they were going on vacation. I did not see that as a problem, but the universe had other plans. On the following Monday (September 30) I received a call from one of Montel's producers informing me that my taping had to be moved up to the following day.

I mentioned the status of the couple who were very interested, but that did not make a difference. They instructed me to have just the one young woman come to the studio and they would provide other guests with their own past-life experiences.

On Tuesday, October 1, the taping was held at Television City. My patient Lori was regressed live into a past life and progressed forward into the 31st century in a future life. The following is a shortened version of what she stated on the tape:

Dr. G: What is your name?
Lori: Blue Eagle.
Dr. G: What is your occupation?
Lori: I am a seer from my tribe.

Lori described a very spiritual life as a seer in Utah during the sixteenth century. She was a male Native American, tall, slim, and muscular, with long black hair. I moved her forward to an event she would consider significant.

Dr. G: Blue Eagle, where are you now?
Lori: I am flying as an eagle. I fly to get a different perspective.
Dr. G: What happens then?
Lori: I am able to communicate with other people.
Dr. G: How do you communicate with these other people?
Lori: With mind.

Lori described a superconscious mind experience in which she left the body and took the spiritual form of a blue eagle. From this astral plane, she (he) could communicate telepathically with another tribe.

Montel interjected a question to establish the time frame.

M: What year are you in?
Lori: It's 1586.

Lori was also progressed into a future life during the thirty-first century.

> Dr. G. What is your name?
> Lori: Julie.
> Dr. G: What year is it, to the best of your knowledge?
> Lori: 3070.
> Dr. G: What kind of work do you do?
> Lori: I am an astronomer.

Lori was then progressed to the significant event of her future life.

> Dr. G: What do you perceive?
> Lori: Well, I've gotten some kind of recognition for my work. My husband does the same work, and he is also recognized. I next progressed her to the last day of her life.
> Dr. G: Now, Julie, tell me what you perceive.
> Lori: I was not expected to die. I'm dying very young.
> Dr. G: How old are you?
> Lori: Forty-five.
> Dr. G: What is it you are dying from?
> Lori: I'm in a collision in space.
> Dr. G: Is your husband with you?
> Lori: No, I'm alone.

Lori, as Julie, described a society that needed its consciousness raised. English was the universal language, and though there were no wars, much tension existed in the business world.

Lori also mentioned some of the age progressions we had done about 1 1/2 years before concerning her future in this life. Some of the experiences she had perceived then had already occurred since I last saw her. She stated that among the benefits she received from being regressed were the ability to know herself at a deeper level and a significant improvement in her self-image.

The main reason for describing the details of this taping rests in the fact that Montel's show was taped in Television City (it has subsequently moved to New York). Television City is the West Coast headquarters of CBS television. When a taping is being held, closed-circuit monitors are available throughout this Pentagon-like complex. Just as Alex's producer was presenting the Grace Doze concept to the network executives, a secretary came in to state that this very topic was being taped on Montel's show. The network executives were not aware of my scheduled presence on Montel's show.

They all watched my past-life regression of Lori. I'm sure there were many other factors involved in approving my project, but as my late grandmother used to say, "It couldn't hurt." The presented documentation stimulated CBS to have a thorough investigation of the facts concerning the Grace Doze case compared to Ivy's statements.

In 1992 a three-week research into police and newspaper reports confirmed twenty-four separate statements that Ivy made. The only two "errors" she made were in saying that she, as Grace Doze, was thirty-two years old when she was murdered, and in constantly referring to her three-year-old son as Cliff. Newspaper reports repeatedly listed her as being age thirty at her death, and referred to her son as Chester Jr. The permission of the governor's office is required to obtain birth and death certificate records of someone in New York State unless you can prove that you are a family member. Even a family member would have to make this request in writing.

The appropriate records were obtained by the independent researcher, and two interesting things emerged. For one, Grace Doze was indeed thirty-two years old at her death and her son's name was Clifford C. Doze (the C probably standing for Chester). Second, nobody had requested these records from 1927 through 1992 until the researcher did. Ivy was not a family member of the Dozes. She couldn't possibly have obtained the birth and death certificates, even through an agent, as a requisition would have had to be completed and would have been on file with Albany.

The material I supplied Alex as the teleplay writer came from my book, *The Search for Grace*. In early 1994 the various production teams were being organized and on May 17, 1994 (the 67th anniversary to the hour of Grace Doze's death) CBS aired *Search for Grace*, starring Lisa Hartman Black and Ken Wahl. Richard Masur played my persona. It took nearly three years, but my creation finally became a reality. As a side note, CBS taped a three minute news "up close and personal" segment on me that aired on the 11:00 PM news following the movie in many cities.

I can't promise you a movie for television, but I can assure you of a greater say in your destiny by following the recommendations given in this book.

Chapter 2
Destiny Vs. Fate

Throughout history there has been confusion between the concepts of "fate" and "destiny." One definition of destiny in Webster's unabridged dictionary is "that which determines events by either necessity or of a supernatural nature." This same publication defines fate as "the power to determine the outcome of events before they occur. This is inevitable and unchangeable by man."

I will differentiate between these two terms by emphasizing the principle of destiny versus that of fate. Whereas we feel victimized by fate and caught in its web, destiny will be applied to a free and flexible influence over our future. Destiny is our purpose or destination, what we choose to be and do, our prime intention in this life. We fulfill our destiny by exercising our free will.

By converting your previous concept of fate to destiny, the first step toward empowerment is achieved. In Greek and Roman mythology there were three goddesses of Fate who controlled human destiny. They were:

- Clotho, who spun the thread of life
- Lachesis, who determined how long man lived.
- Atropos, who ended human life.

The word fate originates from the Latin *fatum*, signifying a decree spoken by the gods. The obvious contradiction between fate and free will has haunted mankind since its inception. If all was predestined, why petition the gods with prayers, why offer them sacrifices, why strive for better things to come about? The answer to the ancient question, as urged by the priestly scribes, was silence: "Out of the silence, the magi said, the answer would be made clear: 'The gods love the silent man more than him who is loud of voice.'" Man was exhorted not to search too deeply into the hidden ways of the gods, but to accept their decrees although they might seem unjust, and yet walk in the way of righteousness.

Here we will focus on taking the proverbial bull (destiny) by the horns and gaining the kind services of the good goddess Fortuna or Luck. The development of the concept of free will led gradually to a conviction that an abiding natural and human law, the foundation of an individual ethic with a social or political conscience, existed in man. We can cite Epicurus (342-271 B.C.) who taught that the gods existed but they did not trouble themselves with the affairs of men, and that although subject to the powers of Nature which could be studied scientifically, man yet had free will and was, within certain bounds, master of his fate.

Free will was a concept proposed by those who emphasized self-determinism and saw volition and action as sometimes being determined by the will of the individual and not only by some outside deterministic or materialistic fate; that is, they are capable of being independent of external influence or internal conditions. Here we have the theory known as indeterminism, which holds that it is possible for an individual to choose a course of action independent of the stimuli affecting him, or the motive prompting him at the time he makes his choice.

With the evolution of man's intelligence, the concept of free will and self-determination became established. Nothing in life is static. Our universe is in a constant state of flux, thus allowing the illusions of fate to be replaced by the grandeur of empowerment and destiny.

A Convict Turns Fate Into Destiny

Throughout this book, techniques utilizing self-hypnosis will be described. The case I am about to present is one of the most fascinating examples of empowerment I have ever read. I discuss this in detail so that you can get a true feel for what it is like to be in a seemingly hopeless situation, yet create a most fulfilling destiny out of the ashes of fate.

The novelist Jack London wrote his greatest masterpiece called *The Star Rover* in 1915. In this novel the main character, Darrell Standing, survives the torture of a device known as "the jacket" by using a self-hypnotic technique today called remote viewing. This out-of-body experience has been referred to as "astral projection." London called it the "little death."

This wonderful story was based on the true-life experiences of one Ed Morrell. Morrell's autobiography was published in 1924 and titled *The 25th Man*.[1] Morrell was the twenty-fifth member of a group of pioneer settlers who became outlaws as a result of a land dispute with the railroad. This took place in the San Joaquin Valley and the Sierra Nevada Mountains in Northern California.

Morrell was sentenced to life imprisonment in Folsom Prison but was later transferred to San Quentin. It was in San Quentin that Morrell used astral projection techniques to survive the torture of "the jacket" and eventually led a movement that resulted in reform of the barbarous prison system in many states in America and in Canada.

Jack London conducted a series of interviews with Morrell in 1912 and particularly focused on the torture Morrell experienced in "the jacket" in San Quentin. Morrell was not your typical criminal. He was merely an activist fighting a war against the railroads, which were cheating the settlers out of their homes and land. Consider how you would respond to being sentenced to life imprisonment

---

[1] E. Morrell *The 25th Man* (Montclair, N.J.: New Era Pub. Co., 1924).

with no possibility of parole for the "crime" of protecting your property rights and those of your fellow settlers. As Morrell describes his sentencing:

> "Life!" angrily thundered the judge. . . .
> "Let your fate be an example to other misguided young men who might be tempted to emulate your career of outlawry. The sentence of the Court is that you shall be confined at the Folsom State Prison to hard labor in the rock quarries for the balance of your natural life!"

In Folsom, Morrell was subjected to a particularly cruel torture consisting of being suspended by his wrists from a derrick in the "back alley" section of the prison. His torture consisted of hanging on the derrick for five hours daily for ten days. When not hanging, Morrell simply lay on a cold stone floor. His nourishment consisted of a few ounces of dry bread and a sip of water once a day. His wrists were severely cut from the weight of his body on the steel handcuffs. The guard was amazed at Morrell's resistance to this punishment. He stated:

> "By the heavens, Morrell, you're the first man who has ever stood that in the history of Folsom. They usually go out in ten minutes. And you never whimpered."

Ed was the first man in Folsom's history who ever walked upright from the derrick. After two years of this torture, Morrell was transferred to San Quentin.

Morrell was placed in the dungeon in San Quentin and one of the guards, the "One-Eyed Pirate," introduced Morrell to a torture device called "the bloody straightjacket" which later was simply referred to as "the jacket." Morrell was the first victim of "the jacket." He was accused of possessing knowledge of firearms hidden in the prison, and this torture was used to extract that piece of information. The Pirate was convinced Morrell was holding out on him:

> "You are biding your time playing a waiting game in the hope you will wear down the prison officials and make them believe you are innocent. After your release, then the fireworks!"

The prison officials sentenced Morrell to thirty-six days in the dungeon on bread and water. Later he was confined to solitary for the rest of his life. The cruelties that history reports of the Spanish Inquisition, the Chinese practice of chopping off the hands and feet of condemned prisoners and the Malaysian method of pouring oil on their victims and setting them on fire carried over to the American prison system in the early part of the 20th century.

During "the jacket" torture, Morrell was gagged and had to endure his bodily excretions, over which he had no control, eating away at his bruised limbs. Numbness was all Ed could feel in fingers, hands and arms. On one occasion

Morrell spent four days and fourteen hours continually in "the jacket."

The universe's test of the inherent goodness of Morrell's makeup consisted of this terrible torture and the intense suffering in order to annihilate his old self and prepare him for his destiny, which was to provide a very special service to humanity.

He described an early experience of astral projection as follows:

> "Mine was a strange sleep. I seemed to be awake and yet I was dreaming. I was conscious of the nearness of friends, a host of them, and yet no living being could enter that dungeon save my natural enemies.

> Suddenly I felt myself being led. Voices commanded me and I did their bidding without hesitation. Without fear or protest I performed many daring feats and passed thru unimaginable tests of bravery. It was like going thru the rites of a weird initiation."

After this initial disorientation, Morrell became aware of a great job. He was no longer in the dungeon of San Quentin but over-looking a vast ocean with the sun glancing on the crests of rolling billows. It was at this time that Ed heard a distant voice saying:

> "You have learned the unreality of pain and hence of fear. You have learned the futility of trying to fight off your enemies with hatred. You

have seen that your sword of defense was double-edged, cutting deeply into your own vitals rather than overcoming the evil that has been working against you.

"From today a new life vista will open up, and you will fight from a far superior vantage point. Your weapon will henceforth be the sword of love, and as time progresses and your power unfolds, this new weapon will cut and hew away all evil forces that now oppose you. And to prove the power that envelops your life in this dungeon, even the straitjacket will have no terrors for you. It will only be a means to greater things.

"Your life from now on must be a work of preparation, and when the time is ripe for your deliverance you will know it. The proof will be a power to prophesy to your enemies, not only the day of your ultimate release from this dungeon but also from the prison, when the great Governor of the State in person shall bring your pardon to San Quentin. Peace and love is yours!"

Following this experience, Morrell felt like a new man. His mind became crystal clear and his senses became more acute. His sense of faith skyrocketed and now he was imbued with the awareness of a higher power from another dimension coming to his aid. Feelings of hate, remorse and vengeance were excised from his soul. He described more advanced trials at his little death as follows:

"I started concentrating upon the willing to death of my body. It was not as Jack London described my little death, not a willing to die of first the toe and joint by joint and bit by bit the rest of the body, but the entire body at one time. .

.

"Then flashings of light danced before my eyes. . . ."Now my heart apparently stopped beating and there was nothing but blackness. I was asleep, at least physically; dead to all appearances; oblivious to sensations yet mentally awake.

"There was a period of brain enlargement, an expansion of time and space, a receding of the walls of my cell and even of the outer walls of San Quentin, and leaving my old pain-racked body laced tightly in the dungeon straitjacket, I bounded away, no longer held to earth but on a quest through space and an eternity of time."

The Pirate and others continued in their attempts to break Morrell. Ed simply smiled and mastered the power of love. The dungeon no longer represented a place of torment and damnation. Morrell's mind controlled the destiny of his body. He could now instruct his subconscious to leave his body and roam at will, witnessing events occurring in the outside world. Later these sightings were documented.

For example, Morrell projected to the deck of a shipwreck just outside the Golden Gate Bridge in San Francisco. This was a progression into the future as the

Golden Gate Bridge was not built until 1937. He noted a man adjusting a strange apparatus and floating to safety as the ship sank. Morrell later patented such a device as the Morrell Life Saving Suit. In subsequent astral projections Morrell's soul played a part in the lives of people he was later destined to meet, some of whom were to aid materially in his rehabilitation and freedom. On several occasions Morrell followed a certain man in Alameda County for hours at a time. These little death experiences were termed by Morrell his "new life in tune with a power divine."

Morrell could at times travel great distances over deserts, over oceans, mountains and prairies. He particularly favored travelling about San Francisco. Floating above Market Street at first seemed exciting, then Ed found himself walking amid crowds on this busy street. The unhappy people he saw affected him strangely, and he kept his distance from the city people in future trips.

Ed described a trip to a Sunday church service in San Francisco as follows:

> "One time I entered a large and beautifully lighted church. I was drawn there by the sounds of the organ. The congregation was standing, singing a hymn; and fearful of disturbing them in their devotion I stole along through the main aisle looking for an empty seat.
>
> "I found one beside an elderly woman, up near the railing. She was singing in a rich, well-trained voice. All through the service I was conscious of her presence and registered how

happy she made me feel. Still, I did not lose a word of the pastor's sermon or any of the wonderful singing of the choir, and I felt that I wanted to stay there forever. To me, that church was a shrine of peace and love."

One fateful day Morrell traveled out of his body to a schoolhouse in San Francisco. He tried to apologize to the teacher for interrupting her class, but she did not register his presence. His attention was focused suddenly on a young twelve-year-old girl sitting to the right near an open window with her head bent low over a book.

When he approached the girl, she raised her head as if to acknowledge Morrell's presence. He described his introduction to this girl as follows:

"When I entered the class room I noticed that just a few of the young faces were cloudy, almost in shadow. But the little girl, my little girl whom I picked out from among all of them, was fairly radiant with light. Her blue eyes were frank, open, and trusting, and she had a sweet smile that encouraged confidence.

"In a vague instinctive way, I knew we were not strangers. Still she was startled at my sudden appearance. I feared that she might lose her poise and hurried to say a few reassuring words. She moved over in her seat. It seemed to be an invitation to sit down."

But something unusual happened following Morrell's prophecy concerning his release. His ability to project himself beyond the walls of San Quentin ended. He could roam about the prison in spirit, but could not venture outside its walls. He did keep the image of that schoolgirl in his mind to detach himself from the excruciating pain his physical body was undergoing.

Morrell made the following prophecy to Pirate shortly after being released from the jacket:

> "Just one moment, 'Pirate,' I have a little prophecy to make, . . . This is the last time I will ever be tortured in the jacket! One year from today I will go out of this dungeon never to return to it; and better still, four years from the day I leave the dungeon I will walk from the prison a free man with a pardon in my hand. More, the Governor of the State will bring that pardon in person to San Quentin!"

Soon after this experience a new warden took charge in San Quentin. This was the very same man Morrell had followed in Alameda County on several of his astral trips. Aside from this, Morrell had no previous exposure to this man. This new warden revoked Morrell's previous sentencing to the dungeon and placed him in a regular cell. Morrell weighed only 96 pounds and was finally able to be in a position to regain his health.

Ed was appointed head trustee of the prison. This was the most responsible position a convict could hold in prison. It carried nearly as much power as the warden himself had. Other prison officials objected vehemently to Ed's appointment, but to no avail.

Four years later the rest of Morrell's prophecy was fulfilled. Lieutenant Governor Warren P. Porter, then Acting Governor of the State of California, presented Morrell with his pardon on the night before Morrell's release.

Morrell described this scene by stating:

> "The scene was ordinary until the Governor spoke. They did not know that a great bond of friendship existed between us, and his words were a surprise.
>
> "With his hand resting upon my shoulder he said solemnly, 'Ed Morrell, here is your pardon! God in his mercy knows you have earned it! In giving you your pardon I do not know of anything in the world that could make me happier. Tomorrow, when you step through that gate to liberty, with all your rights as a citizen restored, I know you will make good. Your sterling character and ironbound determination must spell success for you. There is a great work ahead and the world is waiting!'"

In 1912 Morrell visited Jack London for a few months at the London ranch in the Valley of the Moon. Here London compiled the material for his novel *Star Rover*. Not only were the heroic efforts and character of Morrell detailed in

Jack's masterpiece, but also the horrors of the entire American penal system.

Some years after his release, Morrell met a friend of his in San Francisco. Another meeting was arranged for later that evening. When Ed rang the doorbell at the specified address a young woman of eighteen answered the door. She was the schoolgirl Morrell visited while in prison. This twelve, year-old girl had grown up to be the woman Morrell fell in love with and married. He relates this synchronicity by stating the following:

> "'I have known you always,' she said. 'The moment I opened that door I recognized you as the man in stripes who had come to me in a vision in the school- room. It is surprising but I have felt your influence guiding me from that day to this.'
>
> "I was happy beyond measure, but a thousand times happier still when she promised to be my wife after her school days had ended. Thus was completed the chain of my prophecies. The last, the best one of all."

Now I trust you can see why I presented this case of fate turned into destiny. There is a further happy ending to this quest of Ed Morrell. After his release from prison, Morrell went on a campaign to reform the prison system. The press treated him as a celebrity, and his work became known nationally. Morrell designed what was called the Honor System, and with his influence, spearheaded a movement that resulted in Colorado, Arizona, Oregon, Washington State, Pennsylvania and Canada implementing this system.

Morrell spoke to a joint session of the Pennsylvania State Legislature in Harrisburg in 1917. He was the first ex-convict in the state's history to address this political body. His social circle included governors, judges, statesmen, noted newspapermen, poets, foreign dignitaries, psychiatrists and a plethora of other renowned figures of the time. He launched The American Crusaders for the advancement of "The New Era Penology" with headquarters in Montclair, New Jersey.

Arizona Governor George W. P. Hunt wrote the foreword to *The 25th Man*. In it he states: . . .

> "When a man has been tortured well nigh unto death, and punished for things of which he was not guilty, and then has been able to rise above the baser human passions and forgive his enemies, he has achieved a victory that the ordinary man finds it difficult to understand. . . . His victory over a barbarous prison system is tremendous. The contribution of Ed Morrell to society in calling attention to the cruel, inhuman and utterly indefensible prison system, is a service that only men like him are competent of rendering."

Ed Morrell summarizes his life's purpose as follows:

> "I not only projected my mind through the power of self-hypnosis out of the dungeon and

into the big living, moving world of today, influencing the lives of some who were destined to play a great part in my future life. . . I was privileged in the dungeon to understand many strange complexities of my checkered career and the purpose for which I had been marked for suffering. . . . . I am satisfied that I have lived and suffered for a purpose."

Ed Morrell's life may sound like some metaphysical anomaly. Do not make that assumption. His ability to see into his future and empower himself is attainable by all. You may not experience remote viewing (astral projection) during your hypnotic exercises, but you will be able to control your own destiny.

These events that helped Morrell weren't simply coincidences, but actual synchronicities directed by Morrell with cooperation from the universe. You will note that his loss of hatred and vengeance and adoption of love, as well as a belief in a higher power, coincided with his miraculous transformation.

My methods do not require such a conversion. This is not a twelve step AA program. It is just one step, empowerment. You can maintain your current religious and political convictions as well as other paradigms and still custom design your own destiny using these techniques.

If Ed Morrell can do what he did, custom designing your own destiny by following the simple recommendations I present should be "a piece of cake." Failure to apply these techniques may very well result in some time in "the jacket."

Chapter 3
Self-Defeating Sequences

In order to accomplish anything in life you must establish a solid foundation. A politician refers to his core constituents as a base. Bridges and buildings are built on a well-engineered and solid foundation. The Great Pyramid of Giza in Egypt has lasted for at least 4,500 years!

Psychologically, communication skills and levels also must be firmly established for any type of relationship not just to survive, but also to grow. This applies to both personal and professional relationships.

In this chapter we will discuss the tendencies people have to sabotage their lives by the things they do or say, or what they don't do or say. I introduced the term *self-defeating sequences* (SDSs) in my first book, *Past Lives——Future Lives*. As I stated in *Past Lives——Future Lives*:

"Since basically all of my patients present themselves with an array of self-defeating sequences (SDSs), it is critical to remove these blocks before any long-lasting progress can be achieved. Good examples of self-defeating sequences are procrastination, lateness, compulsive spending, alcoholism, over-eating, impatience, etc. One tends to create difficulties in one's life (and lives) that prevent one from achieving desired goals, whether personal or professional. The self-image (how we perceive ourselves, not how others perceive us) is lowered. The first step in hypnotherapy is to improve this self-image. If you build a house on quicksand, it won't be around to benefit by appreciation. I have already discussed the use of cassette tapes personally recorded by myself for my patients to help establish a sound and strong psychological foundation."[1]

Building up the self-image and establishing higher levels of communication is what this chapter is all about. In order to accomplish these all forms of procrastination and other SDSs must be removed.[2] When I see patients in my Los Angeles office, I assume three factors are present in their psychological profile:

---

[1] B. Goldberg, *Past Lives——Future Lives* (New York: Ballantine, 1988). pp. 167-168.
[2] Ibid.

- Poor self-image.
- Self-defeating sequences (SDS).
- A history of victimization.

By improving the self-image, the other two factors will be removed. Uncovering the truth about yourself and the universe is one of the first steps in this process:

- Undesirable circumstances in your life result from a masking of the truth.
- Listen to your impulses (subconscious), because they are the truth.
- False beliefs act to hide the truth.
- You must remove from your life anything that causes the truth to be hidden.

Communication is an evolving process. The most important type of communication is that which you establish with your subconscious. The hypnotic exercises presented in the next chapter and throughout this book will assist you in that endeavor.

A poor self-image creates vulnerability to fears and this progresses to procrastination and immobilization. Our conscious mind then uses defense mechanisms (rationalization, intellectualization, displacement, sublimation, etc.) to create self-defeating behaviors in order to justify these responses and negative programming.

We can avoid these potential problems and custom design our destiny by employing optimistic thinking (positive mental tapes), affirmations, and visualization techniques. Music can greatly enhance the successful application of these methods. Two additional prerequisites to success are perseverance and faith in yourself.

Since procrastination is by far the most common SDS, let us discuss this in detail. I have never worked with a patient (and I have seen over 11,000 individuals in my practice) who was not afflicted with some form of procrastination.

Procrastination

Procrastination is simply avoiding something by putting it off. There are many reasons for this putting off for tomorrow what you could do today. Your rational mind (the defense mechanisms or conscious mind proper) is quite expert at formulating excuses for these delays. What is interesting to note is that most of the activities that are put off represent no real problem once they are begun. It's the initiation of the chore that is the problem.

Most people delude themselves into thinking they are not compromising their goals by putting something off because they can always do it in the future. This especially applies to dealing with tasks or people that you find difficult or unpleasant.

It really boils down to avoidance. Procrastination is simply coal for the avoidance furnace. Boredom is another common aspect of this SDS. Life really is quite interesting, but it is the conscious, freewill choice of many to be bored. Because boredom is characterized by an inability to spend the present in a personally fulfilling way, it becomes one of the negative consequences of procrastination. To deal with this, individuals may devote their time to some hobby or other immediate gratification activity (such as overeating) to eliminate boredom. This becomes a vicious cycle and procrastination is now embedded in their behavior.

Don't complain about the world or your life. If you want something or someone to change, do something about it now. Be a doer, not a whiner, a critic, a hoper nor a wisher. Be empowered.

SDSs always result in some form of failure. This may be a failed relationship, business or other desirable goal. There are many ways to fail, and it is important to discuss the manifestations of SDSs. The following are some of these manifestations:

- Lack of self-discipline. This is based on your self- image.
- Indecisiveness. The lack of a decision is itself a decision. The problem is that this type of inaction almost always results in failure.
- Difficulty in relationships with others. The single most important quality in life necessary to succeed in any endeavor is the ability to get along with your fellow human beings.
- Making decisions by simply guessing or applying snap judgments based on emotions, rather than by a conscientious effort of fact gathering.

- Letting your ego or vanity determine your actions.
- Lacking a specific and well-defined game plan.
- Insufficient education, whether formal or other, in the field for which you chose to devote your professional time.
- Lack of motivation and ambition to improve your condition.
- Poor health due to factors well under your control. Such things as proper exercise, diet, abstinence from drugs and other compulsions are well within your direction.
- Lack of integrity. It doesn't take long for unethical and illegal behavior to be made known in any industry, but especially in personal relationships.
- Fear of taking calculated risks. Either exercising too much or using too little caution is a formula for disaster.
- Lack of tolerance for the opinions or deficiencies of others. By learning to motivate and improve the performance of others, you will avoid many failures.
- Choosing a field of work that you do not like, and lack of enthusiasm.
- Being a jack-of-all-trades. Become focused and knowledgeable about certain areas. You can always hire or consult with experts in any area.
- Impetuous spending habits.

- Poor selection of business associates. Whether an employer or employee, everyone you surround yourself with in your life is a reflection of yourself.
- Procrastination.
- Lack of follow-through on goals.
- Cynical and defeatist thinking.
- Poor selection of a mate. Your significant other must be supportive of your goals and in general, compatible with you.
- Insecurities particularly characterized by fears of failure, as well as other fears.
- Inability to separate your personal life from your professional activities. You may succeed in business but one day you will come home to an empty house with a disparaging note on the bathroom mirror.

Perseverance

One must develop perseverance in order to move forward with goals. It is a form of emotional paralysis emanating from anger, frustration or fear that results in a person becoming a victim and simply giving up. Empowered souls persevere without this reaction.

The basic theme of a victimizer is to wear down the victim. If put off long enough, over eighty percent of the protesting public will withdraw from the field. Lawyers daily with lawsuits and continuances utilize this technique.

Custom Design Your Own Destiny

When you custom design your own destiny, creative solutions will come to you allowing you to accomplish your goals with minimal involvement of time, energy and money. Naturally, you will have to exercise good judgment to choose your battles. You can't fight the world and waste precious resources over every little issue in your life.

When you raise your consciousness (see chapter 14) the universe will reward you with fewer of these annoying tests. If you persevere and follow up tirelessly, never even entertaining the idea of being put off, then you will almost always emerge not only having reached your goals, but often having far exceeded your initial expectation as well.

As a personal note, I received 48 rejections on the manuscript for my first book, *Past Lives——Future Lives*, before a publisher accepted it. Shortly afterward a second publisher made an offer. Persistence most definitely pays off.

In order to establish a solid psychological foundation for taking charge of your destiny, you need to make greater use of our six major positive emotions: enthusiasm, hope, desire, love, compassion and faith. In addition, we must eliminate the six major negative emotions: hatred, anger, fear, jealousy, greed and revenge.

We cannot experience a positive and negative emotion at the same time. The exercises given in this chapter and throughout this book will assist you in programming these negative emotions and replacing them with the positive ones.

Fear

Fear is a major cause of Self-Defeating Sequences. Psychology has long ago established the fact that fear is merely a state of mind. Clinical experience has taught me that there are six basic fears: ill health, criticism, death, poverty, lost love and old age. The worries of most people commonly arise from fear of poverty, ill health and criticism.

Since fears are but a state of mind, we have control over them. The fear of criticism, for example, is a chief cause of procrastination and failure in general due to obsession about what others will do, say or think. The solution is "To thine own self be true."

This may at first appear a selfish philosophy. I have already established the integrity prerequisite for these recommendations. As long as your motives are pure, you need not concern yourselves with the opinions of others. In fact, the more successful and empowered you become, the greater will be the frequency of the jealousy exhibited by other less empowered souls. I refer to this as the PJ (Professional Jealousy) Syndrome.

The fear of poverty is sufficient to destroy your chances of attaining any goal. This form of insecurity:

- immobilizes the imagination
- discourages initiative
- supports procrastination
- results in indecision

- undermines enthusiasm
- destroys self-reliance

This fear lays the foundation for failure. It discourages empowerment, leads to insomnia, unhappiness, and invites all sorts of other SDSs.

Sometimes we are overcome by feelings of immobilization. These can be panic attacks, severe headaches and other psychosomatic complaints. Most of the time these are simply SDSs meant to fester procrastination.

Immobilization is the result of an accumulation of negative emotions. Just like a safety valve installed on a complex piece of machinery we need an outlet for these negative emotions and the stresses of everyday life, or the result is that we become immobilized.

Always remember that life is a continuing series of experiences rather than one isolated encounter. This will help you eliminate the tendency to equate your "performance" in anything with your self-worth. Just because a relationship ends or a job is lost doesn't mean that you are not deserving of happiness and success. Possessing the knowledge and empowerment of your own unlimited potential will allow you to more efficiently custom design your own destiny.

The world around us is constantly changing. There are those who view life as single experiences, and others who look upon our world as continuing experiences. The single-experience proponents are not happy campers because they evaluate their lives by contrast to the fortunes of others. For them others are lucky and live happy lives, whereas these single-experience types have been unlucky and wind up with unhappy existences.

Continuing-experience exponents view life as constantly changeable and therefore something within their control. For them there are always new solutions. Change is welcomed as an exciting challenge. The expression "success is a journey, not a destination" is what they live by.

The tendency to evaluate your life in terms of achievements, trivial or monumental, along the way, destines one to the frustration of always seeking out other destinations. Taking one day at a time and empowering yourself is the way to custom design your future.

Another form of programmed failure revolves around our thought processes. We will deal with consciousness expansion in more detail in chapter 14. For our current discussion let me simply state that failure will result when you develop a failure consciousness. Success will be the reward of those who practice success consciousness. A simple exercise is to change your past assumption of failure to one of success. Expect the best and assume you will succeed in everything you do.

By simple repetition of positive affirmations to your subconscious, you will change the circumstances in your life by attracting success. A thought can actually be converted into material rewards through the application of quantum physics (the new physics). The mechanism is rather complex, but let me simplify it. A thought presented to the subconscious repeatedly is accepted and transformed into its physical equivalent by the most practical means available. This could be attracting a certain person or opportunity into your life that otherwise would have passed you by, had your thoughts been negative. The reverse is also true.

When you add emotions to this equation it speeds up the mechanism. The emotions, or the "feeling" portion of thoughts, are the factors that give thoughts vitality, life, and action. The emotions of faith, love, and sex, when mixed with any thought impulse, give greater action than any of these emotions can do singly.

Since none of us perceives the outside world with complete accuracy, all self-talk is based on distortions and illusions. Our brain interprets the data it receives from our five senses. Just as a newspaper editorial reflects the position of the paper, our mind sees what it wants to see. We may as well slant this distortion to the positive side. You will find the effects far healthier.

Optimistic thinking is characterized by the following paradigms:

> Focusing on the present.
> Always looking on the bright side.
> Expecting a good thing to happen—always
>   expecting the best.
> Being positive about the future. See it in
>   terms of what can be done rather
>   than what cannot.

Perceiving all setbacks as learning opportunities and challenges to be overcome.
Recalling only positive past events.
Viewing all obstacles as temporary and good events as permanent.
Attributing good events to your own efforts.
Generalizing a positive outcome to your entire life. Statements such as, "My whole life is working great, just as I planned it" can be made following a success.

Optimists eliminate the words "should," "ought to," and "must" from their vocabulary. Words such as "want" or "could" are used instead. This removes the burden of guilt and represents an intention upon which you choose to act.

Affirmations

Repeating positive statements known as affirmations represents another method of reprogramming our subconscious. These statements become just as powerful as their negative predecessors over time.

The best way for you to practice affirmations is to create positive statements about yourself and place them in the present tense. Next, set aside a few minutes each day to repeat these statements out loud or to yourself. These statements should be written down. They can be used during visual imagery exercises, meditation or self-hypnosis. Here are some examples:

I am in control of my life.
I am confident and motivated about my ability
   to _____.
I create my own reality.
I can relax at any time I choose.
I deserve success in all my endeavors.
I unconditionally love and accept myself.
I have a calm mind and body.

Music

Music exerts quite an effect upon our behavior. Fast beats make us aroused and alert; slow, quiet music calms and relaxes us; high-pitched music comes across as playful and happy; low-pitched music is associated with serious or sad moods.

Nature sounds can be very soothing, renewing, and relaxing. Sounds emanating from the ocean, the chirping of birds, rain, the wind rustling through trees, the chatter of squirrels, and so on, have a definite effect upon us.

Aerobics classes always use music. Music may facilitate your motivation to exercise, increase endurance, focus your concentration, attend to chores and get in tune with your body. Some upbeat and fast-tempo music makes you feel less tired. I always incorporate music in my hypnosis sessions and on the self-hypnosis and meditation tapes I give my patients.[3]

---

[3] B. Goldberg, *New Age Hypnosis* (St. Paul: Llewellyn, 1998).

One way to select music that is best suited to you is to listen to a variety of music styles. At this time, record which types make you feel happy, sad, energized or relaxed. Now begin listening to these pieces when you feel moody and note your responses.

Healing with sound and chanting has been practiced since ancient times. All forms of religion use music in their services. For thousands of years, lullabies have assisted children in falling asleep.

Music that is used in combination with guided imagery facilitates psychological and spiritual growth. Psychosomatic disorders of all types, including headaches, digestive problems, pain, anxiety and depression have been successfully treated with music.

Music enhances relaxation and learning and aids the effectiveness of other conscious-raising techniques.

The following music selections may be used to assist in your consciousness raising.

> *The Golden Voyage*, Vol. 1 by Bearns & Dexter
> *Seasons* by G. Lee
> *The Magic Elfin Collection* by M. Rowland
> *Crystal Suite* by Steve Halpern

The only real obstacles we have to our growth are our defense mechanisms. These components of our consciousness (conscious mind proper) function to prevent change. To change we must over-come our defense mechanisms.

Here are some of the defense mechanisms that we face daily:

Rationalization: Finding reasons which are not the real ones to make actions, thoughts, or words acceptable to the self-image.

For example ——"Everybody cheats."

Displacement: Disguising a wish (fear or hate) by substituting another object to blame——The wife takes out her feelings against her husband on the child (and the child kicks the dog).

Regression: Resorting to behavior that is characteristic of an earlier age——"I'm going home to mother."

Repression: Subconscious forgetting or simply inhibiting any threatening stimuli——"I forgot my dentist appointment."

Projection: Attributing one's own faults, thoughts, or desires to others; projecting guilt on them——"My father is stingy." (I'm afraid that I'm stingy.)

Withdrawal: Daydreaming to escape reality, pain, responsibility, or decisions; inability to get things done——"People don't care about me, so I'd rather be alone."

Identification: Establishing oneness with a valued person, group, or thing——"I belong to group X and that makes me important."

Reaction formation: Exaggerating the opposite of true feelings——"We've got to wipe out pornography" (enjoys pornography).

Aggression: Hurting and attacking oneself or others either verbally or physically——"The best defense is a good offense."

Compensation: Substituting achievements in one area to make up for weakness in another——"I'm homely so I try to get good grades."

Bad Luck Only Exists In Your Mind

The concept of the subconscious translating a negative impulse into a physical equivalent is the basis of what is commonly termed "bad luck." Empowerment is the only and relatively easy way of achieving a solution to overcoming bad luck.

When you program your mind with a poverty mentality (or other form of SDS), misfortunes will occur. Programming works both ways. Positive programming creates an abundance mentality, which will be translated into its physical or monetary equivalent. This sets up a chain of events that eventually creates a state of expectancy or belief, which in turn modifies your own attitudes and actions and results in abundance (a financially lucrative business deal or a fulfilling relationship).

The key element in this positive cycle is your belief or faith. This determines your actions and functions as the catalyst that will transform a SDS into an empowerment asset. Expect the best and assume that you will always succeed. Program your subconscious with positive affirmations supplemented by visualization exercises and this method cannot fail.

Refer back to chapter 1 in which I described how I created my own reality and custom designed my own destiny in reference to the successful completion of my movie for television.

To facilitate this system it is critical that you immediately substitute positive emotions and thoughts for the negative equivalents that dominate and discourage your subconscious. Faith is merely a state of mind and can easily be established by self-hypnosis.

Always have faith in yourself and some form of higher power. Faith is the basis of all miracles and other phenomena that modern science cannot explain. Faith is the starting point for the creation of financial success. The only way to counteract failure is through faith. Faith is the only method through which the power and force of empowerment can be harnessed and used. It is faith that gives the power and action to our thoughts that permits us to custom design our own destiny and eliminates all forms of SDSs.

There is a type of magnetic attraction to these forces. The energy of our soul and of most of our universe is actually electromagnetic radiation. By raising the quality of our electromagnetic radiation (subconscious) through positive programming, we are in effect attracting equally positive circumstances (also manifestations of electromagnetic radiation) into our awareness.

Any plan, idea or purpose may be placed in our subconscious through simple repetition of thought (programming). This is one reason why it is advisable to write down your goals and state their purpose. A low self-image or host of other SDSs can easily be programmed out and replaced with its positive analog and highly developed powers of faith by this very same approach.

Removing Negative Tapes

You can think of your subconscious mind as a rather complicated computer filled with all sorts of tapes (programming). You can always change the software by turning off the negative tapes. Such negative tapes as, "I'm not smart enough to get that job" can prevent you from obtaining a position you are otherwise qualified for. Only you can initiate this change. The exercises presented in this book must be practiced for this to occur. Reading about them is only a first step; it is not enough. "How do you get to Carnegie Hall? Practice, practice, practice."

Listening for these negatives is the first step. Once you have identified these manifestations of SDSs, you can initiate simple techniques to "head them off at the pass." You just can't ignore them or pretend they don't exist. You must interrupt them, break them apart and destroy them. Utilize such thought-stopping processes as:

- "Get out of here."
- "I don't want to listen to that junk anymore."
- "I don't have time for negativity."

One of the most common forms of these negative tapes deals with fostering feelings of hatred. Hate will immobilize your growth. It is a means by which we punish and destroy ourselves for the actions of others.

Vengeance, prejudice and violence are its equally destructive siblings. It is up to you to form the posse that will "run these varmints out of town." I refer you to chapter 2 and how Ed Morrell's life dramatically changed when he lost his hatred for the prison system and accepted a higher power.

Lose The Complaints

Empowerment is the theme of this book and my life's work. An empowered soul does not complain or whine. When I give workshops I always entertain questions from the audience. My classic response to a whining comment from an attendee in a presentation in Southern California is, "I cannot support your remark. We're in Southern California; the *whine* country is located in the northern part of this state." To be truly happy and empowered requires a complete absence of complaining, especially about the things you cannot change. If you cannot change something, it is a fact of life. Go on to some circumstance you can modify. That is growth.

Two examples of complaints that are most irritating to others are:

- "I'm just too tired."
- "I don't feel well."

Informing others, including loved ones, of these conditions will not help you. It will only result in abusing them. If you are truly empowered you will want to work out these difficulties yourself.

Complaining encourages self-pity and immobilizes you in your efforts to get on with your life, and to give and receive love in your personal life. This useless activity must be eliminated immediately.

If you truly love others, then you would want to take an active role in removing these factors from your life and empower yourself and others in the process. Since only you can remove the cause and effect of these complaints, do what the Nike® commercial instructs, "Just do it."

Exercises To Eliminate SDSs

- *Reality appreciation and acknowledgment. For this exercise take some time out and just observe the beauty of your environment. Focus on the trees, mountains, oceans, rivers and other natural wonders in your locality. This will not only eliminate boredom, but it will sharpen your perceptive abilities and prepare you to use these talents in other situations that will benefit you personally or professionally.*

- *Remove any illusion that your spouse, children, friends, employees and others in your life "owe" you anything simply because they live with you, work with you, and so on.*

- *Firmly acknowledge that you have the power to control and change your attitudes toward anything. Decide now to control your attitudes, rather than be controlled by them.*

- *Eliminate your tendency to analyze, assess, evaluate and interpret the world around you. Replace this counterproductive activity with doing and enjoying exercises.*

- *Concede the fact that there will always be kooks, criminals, snobs, prejudiced people and other personality types that you simply don't like. By eliminating the natural tendency to label them as "bad," remember they probably have an equally low opinion of you.*

- *Alter your own vocabulary and ideas about reality. Pay particular attention to sayings such as:*

  "That person is worthless."
  "It's a lousy day."

- *Correct yourself when any such negativity surfaces. You will change your attitudes by altering your speech and behavior.*

- *Rehearse taking a different perspective from what most people assume. If others are upset by something, that is their right. Do not allow their misery to become yours. You can make a conscious choice (and eventually a subconscious programming change) to enjoy each and every moment of your life. Who says most people are "right" anyway? Look around; do you not observe most people exhibiting unhappiness and being overcome by stress and baggage?*

- *Remove the natural tendency to classify your personal relationships as permanent. Instead, consider them as moment-to-moment encounters renewable by mutual consent. You really can only experience another in this moment. Death, divorce or other circumstances can end this relationship at any time. You will increase both your fulfillment and that of your significant other by eliminating the pressure and obligation of a permanent relationship. Only insecure and codependent people need that type of assurance.*
- *Reduce or eliminate the tendency to react violently or emotionally to the thoughts and behavior of others with whom you disagree. There is no advantage to your becoming upset over their mindset. You will rarely be able to change another by your mere disagreement.*
- *Practice self-hypnosis and meditation exercises, even during your busiest and most stressful days (see chapters 7 and 8).*

The purpose of these exercises is to increase your awareness of your beliefs about reality. If you can change your beliefs and accept and appreciate what the world presents to you, rather than wasting your life judging, evaluating and stressing yourself, you have completed the first step to your own empowerment and custom designing your own destiny.

This next exercise is a simple method for using affirmations and visualizations to effectively alter your belief systems. If you truly allow yourself to accept the belief that you can attain empowerment, then that is the reality you will create. Each individual can choose to focus on and accept whatever beliefs he or she wants.

These exercises are designed to train you in the art of altering your beliefs. Just because in the past you have adopted limiting and self-defeating beliefs doesn't mean that you can't change them at any time. It is only through deliberate and stubborn resistance that you will allow the previously accepted beliefs to continue to be a part of your reality.

Accept the fact that you can accomplish these time-tested techniques. Formulating excuses for not practicing these exercises is part of the old you, and not at all characteristic of an empowered soul. A new future of abundance awaits you as you put your faith in this system, even before you have physical evidence to support it.

You will be far better off if you put aside your doubts for now, and proceed to program yourself to a frame of mind that will be conducive to what you want to achieve. You don't have to completely obliterate your doubts—just put them on the back burner for a while.

Affirmation/visualization exercises are simple and fun to practice. You need only apply them to the new beliefs you have developed for this specific topic. Here is an example of a simple affirmation/visualization exercise.

It is best to develop the habit of practicing this exercise at the same time each day. To thoroughly benefit from this approach, I strongly recommend you practice with any relaxation method you have utilized in the past:

Now breathe deeply and systematically relax your body by any method you feel comfortable. Clear your mind of all thoughts and worries. A simple recommendation is to listen to some relaxing New Age music for a few minutes as you clear your mind.

Now list a set of positive affirmations and visualizations on a sheet of paper. Start with your first affirmation and begin to speak it, either aloud or in your mind. Say it with a deliberate and confident forcefulness. Believe what you are saying as you say it. During the exercise you are to "pretend" that what you are saying is really true. Keep your focus of attention exclusively on the topic at hand. Repeat the statement over and over and then begin using your visualization. Imagine it as vividly as you can. If you are visualizing some desired thing or situation, imagine that you have already achieved your goal.

Allow your imagination free reign during this procedure. During each visualization, see the event leading to abundance actually occurring. Feel the exhilaration and excitement accompanying your success. As an illustration, suppose you are working on changing your beliefs about your ability to make good business decisions. Perceive yourself making a specific business decision and follow it through to illustrate that this was an ethical win-win-win approach that resulted in your benefiting significantly financially, while growing spiritually at the same time. Create a feeling of pride and fulfillment to accompany this visualization.

When you have completed your first exercise, proceed with the second, then the third, and so on until you are finished. Some of these topics require only a minute or two on each. Others may take between five and fifteen minutes for a specific area. Anything over fifteen minutes in any one area is unnecessary. Experience will allow you to develop a practical regimen.

Never underestimate the potential of this technique because of its simplicity. You are unleashing an ability of spirituality that can be used to literally change the course of your life. You've got nothing to lose by giving it a try. It is applicable for conscious creation in any area. When relaxing to do your exercises, realize that spending a few minutes imagining something accomplishes work. When you direct the power of your imagination, you are harnessing the creative forces of nature and putting them to work for you. This is what an empowered person does on a daily basis.

Regular application of the exercises presented in this book is necessary to make the changes in beliefs you so desire. Get into a pattern of daily practice for several weeks. Don't miss a day. Later on, if you skip a day or two, it won't matter. Remember to feel free to update and change your exercises whenever you have reached a goal or simply feel like adjusting them.

A further application of your training will be evident in the early stages of your practice sessions. Your defense mechanisms will attempt to distract you from your goals. These methods allow you to examine your beliefs about these attempts to sabotage your efforts and reshape your ideas as needed. *Do this daily !*

Abundance Visualization Exercise

Practice your favorite relaxation technique and then focus on the following abundance goals:

1.   I will have a minimum annual income or net worth of $ 100K in exactly six months.

2.   My annual income or net worth in twelve months will be $ 150 .

3.   In five years my annual income or net worth will be $ 3 million

4.   My life in the future will be characterized by attracting fellow empowered souls, just like I am. I now see myself in exactly one year doing just what I want to do, attaining abundance and being surrounded by like-minded people.

5.   Repeat these goals for three years, five years, ten years and so on.

This exercise will assist you in removing limiting beliefs about abundance and focus your subconscious on your vision of becoming an empowered individual. You must recognize that committing yourself to abundance goals means investing a certain amount of your energy in income-producing functions.

Devising a game plan with specific goals is necessary for success in this endeavor. Stating simply to yourself "I want to be rich" or "I want to attract my soul mate" is inadequate for realizing these objectives. You must be specific. This book deals with the principle of empowerment. By developing a money consciousness you will accumulate riches. Establishing a love consciousness will bring a soul mate into your life. Focusing on a power consciousness will result in your influence on the world spreading like a California brush fire in July. The choice, as always, is yours.

Chapter 4
Hypnosis As A Way To Eliminate Self-Defeating Sequences

Hypnosis is a natural daydream level that we experience for approximately four hours during each waking day (driving on a highway, watching television, etc.) and three hours during the dream (REM) cycle while we sleep. We thus spend seven hours out of each twenty-four hour day in this state. That adds up to about 2,500 hours each year!

When you are in hypnosis, you are in a frame of mind during which your defense mechanisms (your beta brain wave or conscious mind proper) are set aside and you can accept and respond to certain suggestions. Some refer to this as a state of hyper-suggestibility, or an exaggerated form of suggestibility.

Unfortunately, the term hypnosis was applied by the English physician Dr. James Braid in the early nineteenth century. He incorrectly assumed hypnosis was a sleep state, and labeled this phenomenon after Hypnos, the Greek god of sleep. Under no circumstances is hypnosis a sleep state.

You most certainly are not asleep when you drive a car or watch television. Yet studies show that you are in an alpha state (hypnosis or the subconscious mind) at least twenty-five percent of the time you engage in these activities.

When a therapist or other person guides you into hypnosis, we refer to this as heterohypnosis. Autohypnosis or self-hypnosis is applied to the induction of the hypnotic state by yourself.

The reason we will spend so much time, and already have, on this natural state of mind is that it is the most empowering gift nature has given us to custom design our own destiny. We must use this natural talent in order to reap its rewards.

In the hypnotic state your reflexes are present, although you may feel somewhat disoriented as if you were absorbed in some fantasy. You are fully aware of what is occurring in the world around you and are never in any form of danger.

The single most important mechanism in hypnosis is suggestion. We all are amenable to suggestion. This is how the various media advertisements work to sell their products. Every single person on this planet experiences self-hypnosis for a minimum of seven hours each day.

At the beginning of the twentieth century a French psychologist named Emile Coué coined the expression, "Day by day in every way, I am feeling better and better." This suggestion was more than mere positive thinking. It was applied when the individual demonstrated this alpha state we call hypnosis.

There is much scientific evidence that you can talk yourself into or out of anything by the use of suggestion and hypnosis. This establishes the unlimited potential for the use of hypnosis for improvement, empowerment and the ability to custom design your own destiny.

Basically, hypnosis works by our setting aside the analytical, rational, conscious mind proper (defense mechanisms or beta brain waves that are very resistant to change) and communicating with and reprogramming the subconscious mind (alpha brain wave state and a highly efficient computer).

For the sake of simplicity, we may divide hypnotic susceptibility into five stages. Stages three, four and five are relevant to its clinical application:

1. Insusceptible
2. Hypnoidal— precursor to the hypnotic state— no symptoms
3. Light stage
4. Medium stage
5. Deep stage

The Davis and Husband classification depends on a point scoring system and is the rating scale most commonly referred to in the literature.

Posthypnotic suggestions can be effective at any depth, although the deeper the trance the more likely they are to be carried out.

If your head spontaneously rolls sideways or forward, the hypnotic depth is increasing. Shallow, diaphragmatic breathing usually is associated with lighter stages, while slow, deep, regular abdominal breathing generally is characteristic of deeper stages of hypnosis. Other signs indicative of increasing depth are the blinking and the involuntary drooping of the eyelids. The trembling of the eyelids after closure usually indicates further deepening.

The best hypnotic subjects are imaginative, open-minded, and more intelligent people. You will never violate your moral or ethical code as a result of a hypnotic suggestion. You are always awake when you are in trance (hypnosis).

All hypnosis is really self-hypnosis. The proof of this is easily demonstrated by the fact that, for any reason, you can reject a suggestion, even one that is beneficial for your growth. Hypnosis has three major components. These are:

- Motivation
- Relaxation
- Suggestion

Hypnosis explains many of the faith cures and miracles that have been reported throughout history. The alpha state is a form of soul healing through the *voluntary* acceptance and application of suggestions. I refer you to my book *Soul Healing*[1] for a comprehensive discussion of this concept, along with some rather dramatic case histories.

---

[1] B. Goldberg, *Soul Healing* (St. Paul: Llewellyn, 1996).

Here are some additional principles of self-hypnosis you should know:

- Hypnotic programming works by repeated exposure.
- Absolutely everyone can be hypnotized.
- You will remember everything that you experience during a trance, unless you are a very deep level subject.
- The more determined you are to attain a goal, the greater your chances of success.
- You cannot be forced to do anything as a result of hypnosis that you would not normally do.
- You must also have motivation to overcome the difficulty of which you complain. It is possible to increase motivation by suggestion.
- If a posthypnotic suggestion is used (most therapeutic suggestions are posthypnotic), always incorporate a cue for the termination of the suggestion if it should be ended.
- If the posthypnotic suggestion should not be terminated, be very careful not to inadvertently give a cue for termination.
- A permissive suggestion is more likely to be carried out than a dominating command.
- Work on only one issue at a time when using autohypnosis.

A comprehensive list of the goals attainable through hypnosis is:

- Increased relaxation and the elimination of tension.
- Increased and focused concentration.
- Improved memory.
- Improved reflexes.
- Increased self-confidence and assertiveness.
- Pain control.
- Improved sex life.
- Increased organization and efficiency.
- Increased motivation.
- Improved interpersonal relationships.
- Improved ability to set and attain goals.
- Facilitating a better career path.
- Elimination of anxiety and depression.
- Overcoming bereavement.
- Elimination of all types of headaches, including migraine.
- Elimination of allergies and skin disorders.
- Strengthening one's immune system to resist any disease.
- Elimination of habits, phobias, and other self-defeating sequences.
- Improving decisiveness.
- Overcoming insomnia.

- Improving the quality of people and Circumstances in general that you attract in your life.
- Increasing your ability to earn and hold onto money.
- Overcoming obsessive-compulsive behavior.
- Improving the overall quality of your life.
- Improved psychic awareness.
- Establishing and maintaining harmony of body, mind and spirit.
- Slowing down the aging process.

Self-hypnosis demonstrates that we all possess a power within our subconscious mind, and this inner force can cure just about anything. Whatever the mind can conceive, it can achieve. That is empowerment and the basic premise behind custom designing your own destiny.

An interesting side-note is that in 1958, the American Medical Association Council on Mental Health formally accepted hypnosis. The British Medical Association put its seal of approval on this discipline in 1955. These rather conservative institutions gave further credibility to this marvelous technique.

The nice thing about self-hypnosis is that after you relax both your mind and body, you can now suggest any goal to your subconscious mind. We refer to a suggestion as a posthypnotic suggestion if it is to be accomplished after the trance has ended.

We can reprogram our mind when we establish a noncritical acceptance of new ideas on a subconscious level. Hypnosis is the ideal method to accomplish this reprogramming.

When you receive information from an outside source (other people, the media, and so forth) and you accept it as truth, that's programming. Self-programming occurs when you say things to yourself. The moment you believe and accept it as truth, you have been programmed. Conversely, any time you communicate information that other people accept to be true, you have programmed them. The easiest way to initiate this self-programming is through the use of self-hypnosis.

As we discuss the functioning of the subconscious mind, there are certain principles of mind-body medicine you should be aware of. Here are some key concepts in this paradigm:

1. *The subconscious will be easier to program the more we can distract the conscious mind.* This implies a setting aside of the conscious mind so that we may communicate directly with the subconscious. Hypnosis does just that. Trying to force yourself to make changes by attempts at will power (conscious mind) alone fail miserably. Examples of this are trying to eliminate a habit, or to will yourself to sleep during a restless evening.

Suggestions about who you are bring about more rapid changes in behavior and attitude than those concerning what you do. For example, "I am a financially independent and empowered soul" is more effective than saying "I have the ability to earn a great deal of money."

2. *The body responds to the subconscious mind's programming.* We can trace the cause of any physical problem to the mind. Any emotional response has as its predecessor a thought that conditioned the subconscious to respond in a certain way. We can use this system to properly reprogram the subconscious to no longer interpret certain situations in your life with anxiety and thus build up our resistance to potential stresses of life.

3. *Your expectations create situations that manifest these thoughts.* When we focus on a dominant thought, the universe cooperates by making that possibility a reality. If you are worried about running into a supervisor at work because you came in late, for example, don't be surprised if you see him or her at the water cooler.

4. *It is easier to add more complex programming to the subconscious once simpler suggestions have already been accepted.* This is the basis of hypnotherapy. We use relaxation suggestions both to distract the conscious mind and to allow comfortable feelings to spread throughout the body. Once this has been accomplished it is easier to present more difficult suggestions to the subconscious, and subsequently, have them accepted. Nothing succeeds like success. This relates to the ancient Hermetic philosophy that "like attracts like."

5. *We tend to find what we are looking for.* The subconscious always moves in the direction of our dominant thoughts. It responds faster to suggestions that reflect previous programming or benefits. If you are looking for good in a person or situation, that is what you focus on and will ultimately find. The reverse also applies. Empowered people always focus on positivity.

6. *The subconscious mind's programming stays the same unless a different program replaces it.* Time may heal a physical injury, but it will not bring about a change in what your subconscious has previously accepted. You must take direct action to replace improper beliefs with new ones. Self-hypnosis is the most efficient and effective way to accomplish this.

7. *Our imagination can bring about more quality changes in our universe than any amount of data.* We operate on what we believe to be true. Living your life as if you are a fulfilled individual now will speed up the process of making this goal a reality, even if at this time you possess none of the characteristics I described in chapter 1.

8. *The subconscious tends to move toward pleasure and away from pain.* I am not advocating aversive conditioning, but rather structuring your new programming to present the lifestyle of someone in charge of your life as attractively as possible to the subconscious. This way the subconscious will assist you in your goal, since it

naturally is attracted to suggestions it considers pleasurable.

You can now begin to understand how the subconscious mind works, and how we can reprogram it to attain desired goals.

Self-hypnosis is an automatic process. It is a form of self-empowerment and a shortcut to success and to a customized destiny. While you are now motivated, desirous of relaxation, and in the mood to practice this suggestion approach, try the following exercise:

Now I'd like to have you imagine that your entire body, from your head to your toes, is becoming very, very relaxed. Focus all your attention on the muscles in the toes of both of your feet. Imagine this warm, relaxing feeling spreading and surrounding the muscles of the toes of both feet, moving to the backs of both feet and to the heels and ankles. Now imagine this warm feeling moving up the calf muscles of both legs to the kneecap and into the thigh muscles, meeting at the hipbone.

The warm, relaxing feeling is moving up the backbone to the middle of the back, surrounding the shoulder blades and moving into the back of the neck.

The warm, relaxing feeling is now moving into the fingers of both hands, just like it did with the toes. This feeling now spreads into the back of both hands, palms, wrists, forearms, elbows, shoulders, and neck relaxing each and every muscle along its path.

The warm, relaxing feeling now moves into the intestines, stomach, chest and neck muscles.

This warm, relaxing feeling moves into the back of the head, scalp, and all the way to the forehead.

Now facial muscles are relaxed, now the eyes (which are closed), bridge of the nose, jaws (the teeth are separated), chin, earlobes, and neck. Now each and every muscle in the entire body is so completely relaxed.

Now I want you to imagine yourself having the very best day of your life.

I want you to visualize feeling physically and psychologically the best you have felt in years. Perceive yourself being successful in some transaction or in a personal situation that currently represents an important goal for you.

Take a few moments and allow this imagery to become a part of your reality.

Play relaxing background music for six minutes.

All right, you have done very well.

Whenever you desire to reenter into this wonderfully relaxing state of self-hypnosis, all you have to do is say the number 20 three times -20, 20, 20 - and you feel yourself sinking down into a deep relaxation. Slowly count from one to five and when you say the number five to your-self, your eyes will open and you will be wide awake.

For this and the other self-hypnosis exercises, I highly recommend making tapes. You can use these scripts to make your own self-hypnosis tape. Use New Age music or other music you find relaxing.

For details on making your own tapes I recommend my book *New Age Hypnosis*.[2] You may also contact my office in reference to a series of audiotapes recorded by me to facilitate your use of self-hypnosis.

Rapid Self-Hypnosis

It is not always possible to spend the extra minutes required to do the basic self-hypnosis exercise. To enter into (notice I did not say "under") a self-hypnotic trance state at any time of the day, you can use the following method:

> *Get yourself as relaxed as you can. Take a deep breath and hold it for as long as you can. Let it out slowly and repeat this step.*
>
> *Close your eyes, breathe deeply and slowly and say to yourself (or play this on a tape): "I am going to relax all the muscles of my body . . .starting from my head to my feet . . . a warm and relaxing feeling is now spreading through my body, from the tip of my toes to the top of my head . . .The muscles of my face and neck are relaxing . . . The muscles of my shoulders and chest are relaxed . . . I'm beginning to feel free of all muscle*

---

[2] B. Goldberg, *New Age Hypnosis* (St. Paul: Llewellyn, 1998).

tension . . . My arms feel limp and relaxed . . .The muscles of my thighs, legs and feet are relaxed . . . As I breathe deeply and slowly my entire body is completely relaxed. I feel calm and relaxed all over. 20, 20, 20."

At this time you should be in at least a light level of hypnosis. Think pleasant thoughts and you will find yourself letting go from the tensions and anxieties of everyday life. You can now give yourself any suggestion to facilitate accomplishing a goal, or merely to focus your concentration or creative energies.

As you become adept at this brief induction method, you can shorten it even further and simply take a few deep breaths, say "20, 20, 20" and the words "calm yourself", "relax", "peace" or anything you associate with a pleasant state of mind.

You may also practice these techniques with your eyes open. It is not uncommon to experience a relaxed feeling permeating your body rather quickly, once you get the hang of it.

At no time will you ever be in danger by applying this technique. This includes while driving. Always remember that self-hypnosis is a natural state in which we spend seven hours during each 24-hour cycle. This is as much as you sleep nightly!

The best way to experience hypnosis is to work with a professional hypnotherapist for a session or two. It is not necessary for successful application of the methods described throughout this book but is recommended for those readers who are light level subjects, or who are unsure of their ability to be successful with these simple techniques.

One thing you should also know is that if you were practicing self-hypnosis and an emergency arose, you would have no difficulty in responding to it. If your tape player broke while you were in a good level trance, you would come out of it naturally or fall asleep if it were your regular sleeping time. It is impossible to get "stuck" in a hypnotic trance, regardless of the depth or type of induction. You can remove all doubts about your ability to change, improve and empower yourself and take control of your life with self-hypnosis.

Visualization Techniques

The visualization technique itself is so simple that at first it would seem improbable that there could be such dramatic results. First, you are taught a simplified form of self-hypnosis with a focus on breathing. You are instructed to repeat the word "relax" and the number 20 three times silently to yourself and to let go of tension in various muscle complexes that are typically responsive to stress by focusing on them one at a time. When a state of physiological relaxation has been established, simply visualize a pleasant, natural scene such as a little brook in a meadow or whatever occurs to you. Spend time and enjoy the scene so that you begin to experience the calming effect both of the fantasy and of holding it in the mind.

These various visualizations act to train the mind. We have already seen how they can be used in hypnotic induction and deepening techniques. Once you master this technique, you can create your own "mental movies" to remove habits and phobias from your psyche.

Visual Imagery Exercises

To get control of your life there is no simpler technique than visual imagery. Try these exercises to develop your inner-sensory awareness, which comprises both physical sensations and emotional feelings.

Narrow Image Visual Imagery

Place a small object about 18 inches from you. Sit comfortably, relax and take several slow, deep breaths while scanning the object. Allow your eyes to come to rest on the object. Do not strain to focus on details, rather see the object as a whole. As you continue to relax comfortably, passively reflect on the object for a few minutes. Slowly close your eyes while maintaining your overall picture of the object. Once your eyes are closed, continue holding the general image of the object in your "mind's eye." As you imagine the object do not try to force the image of it on your visual screen, but see the object as separate from yourself.

Keep practicing this exercise until you can retain a clear image of this object when your eyes are closed.

Broad Image Visual Imagery

Relax as above and mentally recreate the face of someone in your life that you know well. Extend this imaginary experience beyond people and picture scenes, paintings and any other subject that comes to mind easily.

After you have practiced broad imaginary visualization several times, begin to practice visualization while you are actively doing things. Then recall these same "photographs" while relaxing at a later time. Having heightened your faculties for visualization to a level at which you can vividly imagine any object, person or scene without effort, the next visual mental exercise helps you expand your inner sensory awareness.

Inner-Sensory Awareness

Relax and recall a place that brings positive memories to mind. This may have been a past vacation or even a childhood experience of the sensations you felt while at that place. If you were in the mountains, remember the smell of clean air and of pine trees, or maybe the sound of a stream. If your thoughts are of the beach, hear the sounds of the surf and feel the warmth of the sand.

Move onto a more complex scene and repeat the above steps. Feel as if you are there at this very moment.

Reference these emotions as you recall in detail this scene and event.

Pay special attention to the details of this scene; the color of a person's hair and eyes, the decor of a room, the movements you and others might imitate. Be sensitive to your surroundings.

By focusing on several sensory perceptions at the same time, you are developing your access and control over your subconscious mind. You can now master the art of regulating your emotional states through subconscious reprogramming. This will in turn influence your physical and psychological behavior.

Imaginary Sensory-Emotional Visualization

Clearly visualize a person you have disliked in the past. Remember your feelings of animosity; actually recreate that negative mental and emotional state. Release all of these negative emotions while you think of this person. When you have exhausted these negative feelings, relax for a moment and allow your mind to go blank.

Concentrate on a person you care for, vividly picture this person and recall all the positive, good feelings you have had for him or her. Make this a clear image on your visual screen. Allow yourself to feel affection. Once again, relax and clear your mind.

Return to the visual mental picture of the person you dislike. Transfer all the positive, good feelings you just recalled to your emotional sensations while remembering the negative association. Actually begin to feel good feelings as you sustain the image of this person.

Try this self-hypnosis exercise to eliminate procrastination, which we discussed in chapter 3. Begin with the rapid self-hypnosis induction:

> *You are persistent, determined and ambitious. You complete each task because you are a success-oriented winner. You fulfill each personal and professional desire in a relentless, yet efficient and empowered way. You have the self-discipline to accomplish all your personal and professional goals. Each day that passes will result in an increase in your self-discipline. You can now complete large and complicated tasks by breaking them down into smaller components and doing each job one step at a time. You are clear and focused on your values and have no reservations about committing to your goals. You remain alert and focused upon what you are doing. You can routinely block out all thoughts except those related to what you are doing. You are a winner and will now always exhibit a success-type personality. You are self-reliant and self-confident. You are filled with independence and determination. At all times you function like an empowered soul. You project a very positive self-image and can do whatever you set your mind to. You evaluate the various factors of a goal objectively and promptly decide what you*

want. You have the courage and inner strength to make life-changing decisions and carry them out. You do what you say you'll do. You finish what you start. You fulfill your commitments. You do it today, not tomorrow. You have the power and ability to do more in less time. You use a schedule and make it work for you. You increase your speed and productivity. You finish your projects. You have the power and ability to create any reality you desire.

End your trance as usual.

Positive Thinking Alone
Versus Hypnotic Programming

There are plenty of books written on the power of positive thinking. Using positive thinking alone without reprogramming the subconscious is bound to result in failure eventually. The conscious mind, or willpower, is the agent involved in positive thinking, and this component of our mind resists change. Willpower is only temporary, as anyone who has tried to overcome a habit will verify.

We must move beyond positive thinking alone and permanently change our beliefs. Only reprogramming the subconscious can do this. This is the reason self-hypnosis is so successful when used properly. Your subconscious, and not the ego, is responsible for creating your reality.

This next script deals with reprogramming your subconscious for positive thinking and actions:

Hypnosis As A Way To Eliminate
Self-Defeating Sequences

You see positive opportunities in everything you experience. Every day, you feel better about yourself. You are optimistic. You are enthusiastic and look forward to challenges. You experience the joy and detach from negativity. Your positive self-image generates success and happiness. You are now at peace with yourself, the world, and everyone in it. You deserve the very best life has to offer. You detach from pressure and retreat to a calmer inner space. You handle your responsibilities with harmonious ease. You accept the things you cannot change, and change the things you can. You are at peace with yourself and the world. You have the self-discipline to accomplish your personal and professional goals. Every day in every way, you increase your self-discipline. You do what you need to do and stop doing what doesn't work. You now adapt and you keep pace with the movements of change. You always consider your options and you always act in your best behalf. You are self-reliant and self-confident. You are filled with independence and determination. You project a very positive image, physically, mentally and emotionally. All of this coincides with a sense of success and motivation enabling you to complete any tasks required of you, as well as those you choose to undertake.

Every day, in every way, you are getting better, better and better. Negative thoughts and negative suggestions have absolutely no influence over you at any mind level.

Now take a few moments and visualize yourself incorporating these suggestions.

Play New Age Music For Three Minutes

Mentally tell yourself that you are going to:
Develop an intense desire for your goals.
Establish a solid factual foundation by doing your homework.
Maintain a high level of cooperation with others in reference to your quest.
Use your own identity and self-reliance (empowerment) skills daily on everything you do.
Be thoroughly organized.
Have a definite purpose and an established game plan as part of your own reality.
Practice saying "Stop!" every time a negative thought or self-putdown enters your mind.
Program yourself to accept compliments and loving gestures from others. Eliminate the skeptical "What's he/she up to?" attitude.
Tell someone you care for, "I love you." Take a risk.
Develop a form of "positive creative aliveness." When you are in any environment, ask yourself, "How can I make this experience a memorable one?"

Remove any illusion that your spouse, children, friends, employees and others in your life "owe" you anything simply because they live with you or work with you.

Firmly acknowledge that you have the power to control and change your attitudes toward anything. Decide now to control your attitudes, rather than be controlled by them.

Eliminate your tendency to analyze, assess, evaluate and interpret the world around you. Replace this counterproductive activity with being, doing and enjoying exercises.

Reduce or eliminate the tendency to react violently or emotionally to the thoughts and behavior of others with whom you disagree.

Say to yourself daily:

I am an empowered individual.

I'm a perennial optimist.

I don't have time for negativity.

I enjoy whatever I am doing.

I build on my successes.

I don't waste time regretting my failures.

I work smarter rather than harder.

I keep my long-term goals in mind even while I'm doing the smallest task.

I always make use of specialists to help me with special problems.

I delegate everything I possibly can to others.

I concentrate on one thing at a time.

I have the ability to concentrate well for long
stretches of time.

I give myself enough time to concentrate on high
priority items.

I have confidence in my judgment of priorities and
stick to them in spite of difficulties.

I do first things first.

I focus my efforts on items that will have the best
long-term benefits.

I keep a list of specific items to be done each day,
arrange them in priority order, and then do
the most important ones first.

I remind myself: "There is always enough time for
The important things." If it's important I'll
make the time to do it.

I don't waste time feeling guilty about what I don't
do.

I end nonproductive activities as quickly as I
possibly can.

I do not fret about time spent on activities outside
my control.

I start with the most profitable parts of large
projects and often find it is not necessary to
do the rest.

I try to find a new technique each day that I can
use to help gain time.

I set deadlines for myself and others.

I consider carefully what is the best use of my time
right now.

I handle each piece of paper only once.

I generate as little paperwork as possible and
throw away anything I possibly can.

Now spend a few moments mentally seeing yourself,
apply each and every one of these suggestions into
your awareness.

Chapter 5
Success Myths

Your definition of success may very well be different from mine and someone else's. The specific definition isn't important. What does matter is that it is based on empowerment and desired goals. In other words, don't settle for less than you can realistically accomplish.

Most people can't tell you what success is to them. Oh, they can focus on money, power and material possessions, but can they state an actual lifestyle and game plan for "success"? Unfortunately, the answer is almost always no.

In the next chapter we will discuss an actual formula for success. This discussion will center on stripping away the myths about this elusive concept.

To derive your own working definition of success, my best recommendation is to practice the exercises presented in Consciousness Expansion (chapter 14). If you would like to formulate such a definition at this time, consider the following suggestions:

- Eliminate all 'shoulds' and 'should nots' from your personal paradigm.
- Follow the lead of your natural instinct or gut feelings.
- Be open-minded and objective in creating your definition.
- Allow room for expansion and a complete metamorphosis of this definition.
- Keep a certain level of personal fulfillment and creativity, as well as growth, a component of this concept.

Life really should, (if you will pardon my use of a forbidden word) be fun. Material success accompanied by personal misery is not my definition of success. Always remember that success is a journey and not merely a destination. The process is as important as the result.

One of the greatest obstacles we face on our road to attaining success is "excuseitis." It is so easy to make excuses for not reaching goals. Such common excuses are:

- "I was not born into a wealthy family, so how can I possibly be successful?"
- "What success I could achieve would not be worth devoting my valuable time."
- "It just wasn't meant to be."

Success Myth #1

A Past History Of Failure Eliminates The Possibility Of Success

The anecdote of Thomas Edison's 10,000 failures before he invented the light would easily put this myth to rest. Other examples can be cited, such as those of Alexander Fleming, Louis Pasteur and Marie Curie. Without these diligent workers and their many past failures, we might not have penicillin, pasteurized milk or radium.

Consider the following rèsumè:

1832 - Lost job and defeated for state legislature.

1833 - Failed in business.

1834 - Elected to legislature.

1835 - Girlfriend died; had a nervous breakdown.

1836 - Defeated in bid for Speaker of Legislature.

1843 - Defeated in bid for congressional seat.

1846 - Elected to Congress.

1848 - Defeated in renomination for Congress.

1849 - Rejected for land officer position.

1854 - Defeated in Senate bid.

1856 - Defeated in nomination for vice president.

1858 - Again defeated for Senate bid.

1860 - Elected president.

Abraham Lincoln did not allow his past history of failures to deny him his ultimate goal. His perseverance can be a lesson to us all. Never allow failure to divert you from your path. Learn and grow from each experience. There are no failures, only missed opportunities. The great football coach Vince Lombardi never lost a game. He occasionally 'ran out of time.' That is the proper attitude.

Success Myth #2

In Order To Be Successful One Must Work Day And Night, Have No Time For A Personal Life And Expend Great Amounts Of Energy.

One of the most common excuses people use to rationalize their lot in life is myth #2. This justification, though easy to use, is quite simply not accurate.

A review of many common examples of successful people will illustrate the fact that they do live complete lives. In general they attend the theater, go to charity functions and socialize quite a bit.

In the beginning of such a quest, more time and effort are required than later on when certain levels of success are reached. If this were not so we wouldn't see as many successful people in all walks of life. Success is actually quite fun, especially considering the alternatives!

I have discussed some of the prerequisites and roadblocks to success in chapter 3. Myth #2 ties in to the procrastination SDS and exemplifies the power of our defense mechanisms. But these defense mechanisms are only as powerful as we make them.

Success Myth #3

**To Attain Success I Must Possess
Certain Extraordinary Knowledge
That Ordinary People Are
Not Privileged To Have.**

Did you ever notice how many books have been written with the "secret of success" come-on pitch? How many speakers tout their seminars and workshops with the tease, "If you attend I'll let you in on the 'secret of success'"? In order for these books and talks to be profitable, one must believe the underlying assumption that there is a secret to success. I do not take pride in bursting bubbles, but there is no one set of secrets to success. Just as there is no one way to hit a baseball, throw a football, market a product, motivate employees and so on. If there were, someone would have bottled it, packaged it or somehow sold it a long time ago.

I have found my secret to success, and you will too. Empowerment dictates that you develop your own secret of success. That's what this book is all about. Custom designing your own destiny is a form of creating your personal secret to success.

The specific knowledge and mechanism to attaining success is lodged within you. The exercises presented in this book have as their purpose an easy way to extract them. Your own Higher Self is the seat of this knowledge.

Do not let others try to sell you the bill of goods that only a special elite can access this knowledge and that the "little people" must watch others succeed, unless they are willing to pay the price.

There are no little people, only oversized egos in control-oriented, insecure souls who prejudicially consider themselves better than you. You need not wear a black armband and yell "power to the people" to comprehend this point. Just sit quietly and think about all the average Joes and Janes who have made it in life. They did not achieve their respective successes by merely buying a book or attending a workshop. They accessed their inner voice and created their own success. You will too.

I do not mean to imply that these books and workshops are worthless. On the contrary, you can learn quite a bit about proven principles and tactics to achieve a desired goal. Just don't become some groupie for a slick sales pitch.

Many successful entrepreneurs will tell you that there wasn't one particular secret they discovered. Hard work, creative ideas, tenacity and so on were undoubtedly part of their success formula, but there was no one secret.

Success Myth #4

I Can't Be Successful Because I'm Not From
A Rich Or Influential Background,
Or Because I Never Went To College.

Expectations play a great role in this myth. Learning to talk is a rather significant achievement for a 1½ to 2-year-old child. The parents expect their child to talk by the age of two, and so it does. Of course, the youngster's vocal cords and nervous system are developed enough to make this feat feasible.

The same principle applies to success. If you don't expect to succeed because you believe in this myth, you won't. But if you do expect to become a success, regardless of your education or socioeconomic background, you will.

Review the résumé I presented on Abe Lincoln. The impressive aspect of his accomplishment was not that he became president, but that he was able to rise above being born in a log cabin, educate himself and seek his own form of success. That required an expectation, belief and a success attitude.

Most of you reading this book come from a middle-class background. You didn't have to walk ten miles to borrow a book as Lincoln did. You most likely have a high school diploma and two or more years of college. Even if you lack college courses, you can still apply the techniques presented in this book to succeed in life.

When you try to focus on myth #4, you will find that there are just too many exceptions to what it represents. No rule or myth can stand with so many exceptions. If you look upon this query with an objective mind, you will find that your reasons for buying into this myth are based on false assumptions. There are no justified reasons for your background preventing you from attaining success, only excuses.

Never forget that as you rise up the ladder of success, you can always hire experts and consultants to obtain information you need. In my own world I am a consultant, and I hire experts when I need certain information. I manage my own successful empire through the very principles presented herein. You can do it all and play both sides of the success fence in empowering yourself.

Empowerment Made Easy

We all have unlimited potential and can most easily become empowered by raising our level of consciousness. I define empowerment as taking charge of one's life, whereas Webster states that it is "man's ability to control natural forces." Perhaps these natural forces relate to our consciousness.

Our multidimensional universe is said to be nothing but a manifestation of a supreme consciousness, the essence of which is love. Our true purpose is to bring this unconditional love into manifestation. Every one of us has a natural tendency to broaden our range of knowledge through curiosity and the assimilation of the experiences we are exposed to in our daily lives.

We all can use consciousness-raising techniques to establish a more equal balance between the masculine, aggressive and logical aspect of our left-brain and the feminine components of intuition, creativity and spiritual orientation of our right brain.

The previous description assumes a right-handed child. Simply reverse this depiction if your child is left-handed. Consciousness can be broken down into the following main categories.

Conscious mind proper. This is our ego, left brain and rational mind that is represented on an electroencephalograph (EEG) as a beta brain wave.

Subconscious mind. Our soul is also known as our subconscious mind and registers on the EEG as an alpha brain wave. This subconscious component is constantly programmed by the conscious mind proper. The subconscious functions as a true computer and usually does not analyze or question its programming.

Superconscious mind. The Higher Self is another name for the superconscious mind. It represents the perfect component of the subconscious mind and is also an alpha brain wave level. Since the last two components of our consciousness represent electromagnetic radiation, the Higher Self has the ability to raise the quality of the subconscious mind's energy to allow it to grow spiritually and become empowered. We will use this mechanism when I discuss self-hypnosis in chapter 7.

I'm sure most people have some idea of how to stay healthy by a combination of diet, exercise and rest. We may understand the psychological factors that exert an influence upon our physical body. Many of us lack a clear understanding of how the nonphysical, spiritual energies in life can affect our health and our ability to deal with the world we live in.

The spiritual energies (consciousness) that continually interact with our physical body dramatically influence our bodies, our thoughts, and our emotions. We don't really understand these forces because they are usually hidden from our ordinary awareness. The purpose of this book is to help bring the hidden spiritual energies into a clearer focus so that you may consciously draw upon them to create emotional, mental, and physical functions in your lives that will allow you to become empowered and fulfilled individuals.

Before I present detailed information about mind-body natural methods to assist in your quest for resolving your problems, a discussion of just how spiritual growth can make this a reality is in order. I like to refer to this as a global assessment, or the big picture. Another term I apply is *psychic empowerment*.

Spirituality As The Big Picture

Spirituality has been receiving increased attention from both health care providers and consumers. Recent literature provides exploration and some clarity in understanding its relationship to health. Spirit is understood to be both the source of and a manifestation of one's spirituality.

Spirituality is a unifying force, manifested in the Self, and reflected in one's being, one's knowing, and one's doing. It is expressed and experienced in the context of caring connections with oneself, others, nature, our Higher Self and God. The key elements of this view of spirituality are the Self and connections. The Self reflects an unfolding life journey that embodies who one is, what and how one knows, and what one does, as well as one's source of strength and meaning. Connections are those attachments and relationships that link Self to others, nature, the Higher Self and God. Spirituality relates to an inner knowing and source of strength reflected in one's being, one's knowing, and one's doing.

The reason many of us fail to overcome our problems is that the energy of desire is intimately woven with the creative power of the soul. The eternal life force that we call the soul (the subconscious mind) gives rise to our creativity, strength, and other capacities that flow from our soul into our personality. When you desire something so intensely (such as watching television instead of doing chores), that feeling of desire stirs up the very powerful soul energies within you and functions to block your ability to create, act, and accomplish in order to fulfill your purpose in the material world.

Those individuals who are susceptible to immediate gratification behaviors have created a climate that encourages the instant fulfillment of physical desires. A certain numbing results from this process of immediate gratification and compulsive behavior through continual fulfillment. For example, if you go forth each day seeking only to fulfill the desire to eat food, to fill yourself with the pleasure of taste and other pleasant sensations of eating, and that is all you do each day, after a while the intense experience of the joy of eating begins to diminish. Then, you attempt to eat more, or you may try to have more intense experiences by eating foods with different tastes. Unintentionally, you set up a cycle in which your search for fulfillment is based upon an experience of satiation, or numbness in your present fulfillment.

A far more spiritual approach is to create a desire to be emotionally fulfilled in profound inner ways that involve love and that bring about the experience of purpose and meaning in life. Compulsive problems and low self-image problems can be eliminated by focusing on the following three areas: (1) learning to bring joy into all other areas of your life; (2) learning to open your heart to love yourself and those around you; and (3) healing your fears by mastering the art of accessing your Higher Self. Successfully accomplishing these three goals will bring you the confidence and trust in your own unlimited capacities of strength, creativity, and love that will help release the desire to substitute addictive behaviors for the true joy and wonders of life.

Another benefit from this suggested regime is that it frees you to utilize your Higher Self to create a more empowered self-image without interference from negative personality patterns associated with a specific sabotaging behavior and low self-image. By daily committing yourself to heal your negative thoughts, feelings, attitudes and beliefs, you begin a change in personality that fosters any goal humanly possible. That is a true form of psychic empower.

Establishing A Spiritual Foundation

What I have observed over the years in my Los Angeles hypnotherapy practice is that those patients who exhibit a more spiritual love of themselves, as opposed to ego, tend to be drawn to the healthy aspects of life they encounter. They will not usually develop such strong desires to engage in self-defeating behaviors. My observation is simply a generalization that applies to the majority of the more than 11,000 individual patients I have worked with since 1974.

There are two modes of subjective experience. The first mode is the inner experience mode—living intensely inside your inner experience and being caught up in your experience. In that mode, you are the creator of your experience.

Mode two is the observer or other experience mode—stepping back from the intensity of your experience to observe what you are experiencing. In this mode, you are the responder to your experience. This allows you to step back from your experience by creating a loving detachment from your subjectivity of the moment, not by numbing your feelings. This detachment is a temporary mode. A continuous use of this mode could result in a loss of intensity of your subjective experience. However, it will be necessary to use this second mode in a limited way in order to fully exercise your capacity to create love in any moment.

This method can be applied after you have learned to make this inner shift in your thoughts and feelings of the moment. Then whenever you desire, you can enter that deeper awareness of your Higher Self, and, from within that deepened experience, you can create feelings of warmth, harmony, and love within yourself. If you attain that capacity and develop it, gradually you will learn that you can also use this ability to come forth to help others create love in their lives.

Nature gives to us through our senses—the smell of flowers, the taste of herbs, the feel of sand between our toes, the sound of waves breaking, the sight of geese flying overhead. For many, the outdoors is a sacred space that calls to and nourishes the spirit. Leaning against a tree, wading in a stream, watching a small critter, and planting a garden are among many paths to spirit.

Consider the following reflective questions and ask them of yourself in assessing, evaluating, and increasing your awareness:

- What gives your life meaning?
- Do you have a sense of purpose in life?
- How hopeful are you about your ability to overcome your problems?
- Will you be able to make changes in your life to accomplish these goals?

- Are you motivated to work at attaining these objectives without resorting to artificial aids?
- How do you feel about yourself right now?
- How do you feel when you have a true sense of yourself?
- Do you pursue things of personal interest?
- What do you do to show love for yourself?
- Can you forgive yourself?
- Can you share your feelings with others?
- What are some of the most loving things that others have done for you?
- What are the loving things that you do for other people?
- Are you able to forgive others?
- What brings you joy and peace in your life?
- What can you do to feel alive and full of spirit?
- What traits do you like about yourself?
- What are your personal strengths?
- What life goals have you set for yourself?
- Do you ever feel at some level a connection with the world or universe?
- How does your environment have an impact on your state of well being?
- What are your environmental stressors at school and at home?
- How do you deal with these stressors?
- Are you concerned about the survival of the planet?

- Do you use relaxation or imagery skills?
- Do you meditate?
- Do you practice self-hypnosis?
- Do you believe in God or a higher power?
- Do you have a sense of belonging to this world?

The heart and soul of spirituality requires that attention be paid to our Higher Self and significant connections. This process implies an ongoing practice of intentional awareness that spirit is present in all relationships. As we become more intentional in our recognition of and response to the spirit present in each relationship, this spirit is reawakened and we can begin to custom design our own destiny.

Chapter 6
A Formula For Success

In this chapter we will discuss factors that will assist you in your goal of attaining success. Most of these are well within your control and will facilitate your ability to custom design your own destiny.

One common characteristic of people who fail in any endeavor is poor planning. In order to establish the control I alluded to in the previous paragraph, you must learn to plan well.

Planning can be thought of as bringing the future into the present in order to do something about it now. Most individuals plan only when under pressure, and they do it rather haphazardly.

Complaints are rampant coming from by those who do not plan. Such comments can be heard as:

- "There is simply not enough time for me to accomplish all of these tasks."

- "I waste so much time doing things that are not important."
- "I'm constantly pushing myself and can never relax."

This is not a formula for success, but a prescription for failure. The first step toward control of your life is proper decision-making.

Empowered Decision Making

The main problem we face in making empowered decisions is to balance our physical, emotional and rational needs. They must all be satisfied, but cannot always be accommodated simultaneously.

Long-term versus short-term goals must also be factored into this equation. If you decide to favor the short-term goal, the long-term benefit may suffer and vice versa.

Before we cover ways to make decisions that will add to your formula for success, let us discuss dysfunctional methods of choice:

- Escapism. Putting off making a decision by doing other things because you are afraid of failing or of what others might think as a result of your taking some action.
- Default. You procrastinate a decision for so long that it becomes too late to make a decision since the opportunity has passed and the decision made is the only one left.

- Habit. You make a decision that is nothing but a repeat of old behavior patterns, whether this works or not. It's equivalent to ordering "the usual" in your favorite restaurant, even though you may not enjoy the selection anymore.
- Spur-of-the-moment. You quickly make a decision because of a deadline or impulse, without thinking or planning about the pros and cons of the various factors.

The main problem with these methods is that there is no plan, no control and no positive payoff. This is not custom designing your destiny, but rather being more like driftwood in the ocean.

Becoming empowered means making good decisions and taking control of your life. The following list summarizes the elements of good decision-making.

- The clear realization that the problem is generic and could be solved through a decision that establishes a principle.
- You can facilitate resolving any problem by first defining it and identifying specifications needed to bring about a solution.
- Thinking through what is "right" before attention is given to the compromises, adaptations, and concessions needed to make the decision adaptable.
- Building into the decision the action to carry it out.

- The feedback that tests the validity and effectiveness of the decision against the actual course of events.

The effective decision maker, therefore, always assumes initially that the problem is generic, or group related. He or she looks for the true problem and is not content with doctoring the symptom alone. Effective decision makers always try to put their solution on the highest possible conceptual level.

The effective decision maker asks himself, "If I had to live with this for a long time, would I be willing to?" And if the answer is "No," he keeps on working to find a more general, a more conceptual, a more comprehensive solution - one that establishes the right principle. The effective executive does not make many decisions. Because he solves generic situations through rule and policy, he can handle most events as cases under the rule; that is, by adaptation.

A decision is a judgment. It is a choice between alternatives. It is rarely a choice between right and wrong. It is at best a choice between "almost right" and "probably wrong." One starts with opinions. These are, of course, nothing but untested hypotheses and, as such, worthless unless tested against reality. To determine what is a fact requires first a decision on the criteria of relevance, especially on the appropriate measurement. This is the hinge of the effective decision, and usually its most controversial aspect.

Finally, the effective decision does not flow from a consensus on the facts. The understanding that underlies the right decision grows out of the clash and conflict of divergent opinions and out of the serious consideration of competing alternatives. To get the facts first is impossible. There are no facts unless one has a criterion of relevance. Events by themselves are not facts.

The effective executive, therefore, asks: "What do we have to know to test the validity of this hypothesis? What would the facts have to be to make this opinion tenable?" The effective decision maker assumes that the traditional measurement is not the right measurement. Otherwise, there would generally be no need for a decision; a simple adjustment would do. The traditional measurement reflects yesterday's decision.

This effective executive is concerned first with understanding. Only then does he even think about who is right and who is wrong. "Is a decision really necessary?" One alternative is always the choice of doing nothing.

The effective decision maker compares effort and risk of action to the risk of inaction.

- Act if, on balance, the benefits greatly outweigh cost and risk; and
- Act or do not act, but do not "hedge" or compromise.

A decision requires courage as much as it requires judgment. There is no inherent reason why medicines should taste horrible—but effective ones usually do.

Similarly, there is no inherent reason why decisions should be distasteful – but most effective ones are.

Formulating Lifetime Goals

Another component of your formula for success is the written statement of lifetime goals. This will help you discover what you really want to do, help motivate you to do it and give more meaning to the way you spend your time.

A written lifetime goal is not a magic wand, nor is it an academic exercise in precognition. This statement is not meant to be a predestined dictum. Properly executed, it will not curtail spontaneity or creativity from your life. What it will accomplish is to focus your directions in life and make them more concrete.

Step 1   Begin this procedure by allotting fifteen minutes for this exercise. At the top of a piece of paper write lifetime goals. List these goals for approximately two minutes. These goals may appear general and abstract but include financial, career, personal, family, community, social and spiritual elements. Now that these two minutes are up spend an additional two minutes making any changes until you are satisfied with your goals.

Step 2   On a separate piece of paper write "The next three years of my life will be spent accomplishing ..." (state three to five years if you are over 35). Repeat the procedures in Step 1.

Step 3   On still a third sheet of paper write, "The next six months of my life, if I should die by the end of those six months, my time will be spent doing ... ."
Do not focus on wills, funerals and the like, but concentrate on the most priority goals to complete. Spend two minutes writing down these goals, and an extra two minutes refining these.

Step 4   Spend an extra two to five minutes reviewing, editing and refining these three sets of goals.

Step 5   Reviewing all three sets of goals should now make it easier to set priorities. Spend one minute selecting your top three goals. Label the most important goal G-1. The second most important goal is now referred to as G-2, while G-3 is the third in priority.
This should be done for each of your three sets of goals (lifetime, three [or three to five] years, and six months). The purpose of this step is to narrow your goals to just what you want to do with your life at this moment in time. These lifetime and immediate goals are to be reviewed and revised periodically.

Now you can closely examine your goals. This form of scrutiny lends itself to being refined, updated, analyzed, pondered, and changed. Committing your goals to paper narrows these paths and facilitates the establishment of priorities.

The following exercise will give you the necessary experience to apply this all-important component of your formula for success.

One goal I hope you include somewhere in your list is what I call "hang time." Hang time stands for hang loose, and this means leaving about one hour each day unscheduled. This free time is to be used to relax from a long day, stressful call, time to catch up with your mail, paperwork, and so on. This will do wonders for the flow of your life and keep it moving slowly and you young.

Daily Lists

This particular aspect of your formula for success may seem obsessive to those who hate lists. This procedure continues where the lifetime goal list leaves off. In addition, this mechanism allows you to plan your day, be more organized and efficient and places you in control of your life.

Remember, you cannot do a goal. What you can do is an activity. These various activities are paths to a goal.

Goals may be short-term or long-term. When you have planned well on both long-term and short-term levels, then goals and activities fit together like well-meshed gears. Most if not all of the activities specified in short-term plans will contribute to the realization of the goals specified in long-term plans.

These daily lists have been referred to as To Do lists, activity lists and other nicknames. I will just call them daily lists. Successful and unsuccessful people are aware of these lists. One difference between them is that the successful types use a daily list every single day. The unsuccessful people rarely or never use one.

It is not complicated to create a daily list. Merely write down activities that you need to accomplish on that day and cross them off as you complete them. You may add others as the day goes on. Rewriting this list is most often indicated when it becomes hard to read.

A more efficient method in this formula for success is to keep a master daily list in your appointment book or other safe place. This is better than small scraps of paper that are easy to misplace. Some of these daily list items may have to be carried over to the next day. Others may require a second effort a week or so hence. The master list assists in keeping track of such items.

Prioritize these activities by assigning an A to the top priority items, a B to the next most important set and a C to the least important activities. It is helpful to use one piece of paper for the A's and B's and another page for the more numerous C's. The A and B paper is kept on top of the C list, and every time you omit the A and B list to do a C, you're aware that you're not making the best use of your time. Items on the daily list may be arranged in several ways. One form is functional: to see, to telephone, to follow up, to think about, to decide, to dictate. Or you can group activities based on the similarity of the work content, the same location, or the same person.

When completing your daily list, do all the A's before the B's, and the B's before the C's. Some days you may get all the items on your list done, but more likely there will not be time to do them all. If you are doing them in ABC order you may not even finish all the A's sometimes. On other days you will do the A's and B's and on other days A's, B's, and some C's.

The important thing about a daily list is to make the best use of your time, not to complete the list. You should naturally complete all the A's and most, if not all, the B's. Some C's will not be accomplished because of time constraints. They can be transferred to the next day or next week, since they are of the lowest priority.

Saving Time

Saving time is also a component in your formula for success. This not only allows you to be more efficient, but it also prevents you from becoming "burnt out" and frustrated.

The following list represents some simple and practical methods I use to save time:

- I set deadlines for myself and others.
- I'm continually asking myself: "What is the best use of my time right now?"
- I recognize that inevitably some of my time will be spent on activities outside my control and don't fret about it.
- I start with the most profitable parts of large projects and often find it is not necessary to do the rest.
- I cut off nonproductive activities as quickly as possible.
- I carry blank paper in my pocket to jot down notes and ideas.
- I don't read newspapers or magazines, and rarely watch television. I do read abstracts to keep up with my fields.

- I skim books quickly looking for ideas.
- I focus my efforts on items that will have the best long-term benefits.
- I try to enjoy whatever I am doing.
- I'm a perennial optimist.
- I build on successes.
- I give myself enough time to concentrate on high-priority items.
- I have developed the ability to concentrate well for long stretches of time.
- I concentrate on one thing at a time.
- I delegate everything I possibly can to others.
- I always make use of specialists to help me with special problems.
- I try to find a new technique each day that I can use to help gain time.
- I don't waste time regretting my failures.
- I don't waste my time feeling guilty about what I don't do.
- I have confidence in my judgment of priorities and stick to them in spite of difficulties.
- I ask myself, "Would anything terrible happen if I didn't do this priority item?" If the answer is no, I don't do it.
- I keep my long-term goals in mind even while doing the smallest task.
- I always plan first thing in the morning and set priorities for the day.

- I keep a list of specific items to be done each day, arrange them in priority order, and then do my best to get the most important ones done as soon as possible.
- I generate as little paperwork as possible and throw away anything I possibly can.
- I handle each piece of paper only once.
- I write replies to most letters right on the piece of paper.
- I keep my desktop cleared for action, and put the most important thing in the center of my desk.
- I give myself time off and special rewards when I've done the important things.
- I do first things first.
- I work smarter rather than harder.
- I remind myself: "There is always enough time for the important things." If it's important I'll make the time to do it.

Beliefs

The last major component to your formula for success is in the form of beliefs. Beliefs can be simply defined as ideas about the conditions of your reality that are accepted as fact. These aren't necessarily accurate depictions of the world. You can actually change your reality by changing your beliefs.

A myth is nothing more than an erroneous belief. In chapter 4, I delineated four such myths of success. A limiting or falsely based belief pigeonholes you for failure. It can literally shape the circumstances of your life. The solution is quite simple. Change your beliefs.

The first objection that comes to mind is, "How can I be held responsible for circumstances that are beyond my control and that resulted in a missed opportunity?" For example, let us assume you have an important interview for a desirable job.

You have spent weeks arranging this all-important interview. Preparations have been made on your part to land this job. The morning of your interview you have an accident (fall in your bathroom, car accident and so on) that prevents you from attending this interview. The position is subsequently given to another candidate.

Are you not simply a victim of circumstance? The fact is that your doubts (lack of belief in yourself or a belief that you weren't qualified for this job) created the circumstances that led to this "accident."

Your beliefs literally custom design your destiny and define your existence. Your beliefs will be manifested and create factors in your environment that will significantly influence the outcome of events in your life. Inappropriate or erroneous beliefs result in undesirable events and vice versa.

In the example I presented, the accident prevented you from having to fail in that new job. You lacked the confidence and mind-set to accept that promotion. That was an error in belief, not a reality. However, it created a reality that denied you an earned opportunity. You can create the reality you desire by maintaining the beliefs that will automatically bring about those positive results and thereby custom design your own destiny.

This is not merely positive thinking. Positive thinking by itself will not work. The problem with positive thinking is that you are using the conscious mind proper or defense mechanisms, whose purpose is to block all attempts to change.

When you change your beliefs, you are correcting the true source of your difficulties, which is the reprogramming of the subconscious mind. It is your subconscious mind, not the defense mechanisms (rationalization, intellectualization, sublimation, etc.) that exert a greater control on creating circumstances in your life. Both minds can and will create these circumstances, but the subconscious mind is much stronger. The defense mechanisms initiate at best a temporary change by positive thinking alone.

Normally the subconscious mind is programmed by the defense mechanisms, and this results in an endless change of false beliefs. By reprogramming the subconscious mind through the use of self-hypnosis, we can now more effectively replace insecure and erroneous beliefs with empowering ones.

The fact that your previously, and probably currently, held beliefs have existed for many years is irrelevant. You can reprogram your subconscious mind in a matter of days with properly administered self-hypnotic instructions. The new physics supports this concept of creating your own reality through the reprogramming of consciousness.

You most definitely possess the means for changing your beliefs. This results in your having control over your reality and the ability, should you exercise it, to custom design your own destiny.

Do not harass yourself for previously contributing to your past frustrations and failures. Remember, tomorrow is the first day of the rest of your newly empowered life. These failures due to then held beliefs will not be repeated now or in the future if you practice the exercises in this book.

The easiest way to alter your beliefs is, first, to formulate specific lifetime goals as I discussed earlier. Second, you can live the rest of your life, beginning today, in a manner reflective of the new empowered you. In other words, act like the powerful and influential executive you will become. Adopt the manner of a CEO, even if you work in the mailroom.

This is not delusional behavior I am recommending. This is empowerment. You do control your own reality, and you can change it into whatever situation you desire. The best way to enact this technique is to use visual imagery for between ten and twenty minutes each day and create your ideal future

When I recommend the use of self-hypnosis, you need to understand that this natural daydreaming state of mind is a suspension or alteration of beliefs. In order to accept any suggestion, the subjects in (notice I did not say under) hypnosis must accept the belief that they are in this alpha brain wave state commonly called a daydream.

Every time you say something negative to yourself with a conviction in the quality of the source, it becomes fact. This fact is later transformed into an invisible but destructive belief and now really becomes a part of your programming. Fortunately, this fact is reversible through self-hypnosis.

Here is an example of how false beliefs can lead to failure. On the following figure connect the nine circles using four straight lines without removing your pen from the paper.

The solution to this task is illustrated by the figure below.

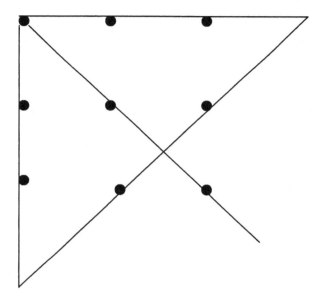

You will note that I connected the nine circles without removing my pen from the paper and with just four straight lines. The key was to go outside of the enclosed box. Just about everyone assumes that one has to stay within the confines of the box.

The erroneous belief that you had to stay within the enclosure of the box housing the nine circles doomed you to failure. You accepted that unwritten rule as fact and it led to frustration. By restructuring your beliefs so that you make the rules (that aren't in violation of the instructions in my example) you empower yourself, discard false beliefs, change the facts to ensure a success. You have just custom designed your own destiny.

Children are the best examples of this principle. Let us consider little Jimmy, who is an A student in the third grade. His family, friends and teacher refer to him as a smart boy.

Jimmy may be exposed to the false belief that good students are not athletic, so Jimmy doesn't play sports with his friends. By keeping away from such pursuits, his friends develop their motor skills at a faster pace. This becomes a vicious cycle for Jimmy, and his futile attempts in later years with classmates or friends who are more athletic than he reinforces his false belief.

This problem can be easily solved by Jimmy engaging in athletic endeavors. He would need to reprogram his subconscious mind to remove those prior false beliefs, but that is just a matter of a simple exercise. Jimmy may require some time to bring his athletic prowess up to that of his contemporaries, but with the proper belief system and empowerment, it is just a matter of time.

When you possess the appropriate beliefs, success is all but guaranteed. The only time this won't work is if you give yourself far too short a time framework with which to custom design your own destiny.

Never give up in your quest for empowerment. If you do someone else will walk in and capitalize on that opportunity. The more persistent and longer you work in this positive direction, the sooner will be your reward of success.

A shift in consciousness is necessary and will be discussed in greater detail in chapter 14. You will find that you can transmit your own faith and persistence to others and get the "impossible" done.

Whatever the mind can conceive and believe, it can achieve.

Most people think success is luck, and they keep trying to win the lottery of life. But success is really the result of planning. It happens where preparation and opportunity meet.

Most people think success is instantaneous. They look on it as a moment, an event, or a place in time. It's not. Success is really a process. It is growth and development. It is achieving one thing and using that as a stepping-stone to achieve something else. It is a journey.

Most people think that success is learning how never to fail. But that's not true. Success is learning from failure. Failure is the opportunity to begin again more intelligently. Failure only truly becomes failure when we do not learn from it.

Chapter 7
Overcoming Fear

In order to be empowered and placed in the position to custom design your own destiny, you must remove fear from your behavior. Fear is a destructive and limiting state of mind that manifests itself as an emotion.

This negative feeling is a product of our mind and is the end product of poor programming. Just as we discussed in chapter 5 concerning the concept of changing beliefs, fear must also be dissected from our psyche.

Fear is an uneasiness of the mind composed of thoughts and it is usually an exaggeration of reality. Whether these are morbid fantasies or well-established facts, it is our interpretation of them that creates the fear reaction. One can then describe fear as an invisible force composed of certain negative and insecure thoughts that surface as an emotion. There are many types of fears, as we briefly discussed in chapter 3. The most global fear is the fear of becoming afraid.

All fears are acquired. Whatever the mind can conceive, it can achieve, including the ability to create or remove fears. Some fears appear to be based on facts or circumstances beyond your control. In reality, your beliefs and your subconscious mind's programming does have the innate ability to exert control over these factors. That is what empowerment is all about.

If you act as a victim to these alleged beyond-your-control factors, anguish, despair and terror will be experienced. Your subconscious mind always has a hand in creating your reality, as we will discuss in chapter 14.

I classify fear as a force because it can lead us to do things that become an SDS. There are two types of people affected by fear enough for it to be manifested as an SDS. The first type is a high-strung type A personality. These individuals are very suggestible and exaggerate most everything in their lives, usually to the negative. Most of their fears are imagined.

The second type is a normally healthy and well-balanced soul who is usually immune to such fears. Occasionally, due to severe loss or real threat to his or her safety, a fear is established. This fear may now be exaggerated as it was in the case of the type A, but this particular fear mechanism in our second type of individual is based on actual facts.

In both of these types of people, imagination runs havoc with logic and rational thinking. It is not difficult to see the role of emotions in this process. "The world is coming to an end," or "I'll die if so and so doesn't get off my back" are examples of this syndrome. In either case, nothing short of a miracle will solve the dilemma.

This chapter concerns itself with fears more than phobias. Although these concepts apply equally to phobias, phobias are even more debilitating. A phobia is an irrational fear and as a retired dentist with thirteen years of practice in that health specialty, I can attest to the effects of these neuroses.[1]

The most important aspect of fear can be applied to its removal. That factor is imagination. Imagination is what transforms a harmless factor in one's environment to a fear-generating stimulus. Take the example of young children who sleep well at night until they see a horror movie on television or in the movie theater. Now they are afraid of the dark and shriek at the top of their lungs at any shadow or strange sound, real or imagined.

It is not always possible to change the facts associated with our fears. What can be accomplished is an alteration in the response to these facts. There are three possible outcomes to the real facts surrounding your fear.

One possibility is that you will be significantly encumbered and never achieve the happiness you seek. In other words, failure is inevitable. Another option is that the disaster you agonize so much about now is not nearly as bad as you suspect.

The last possibility involves empowerment. Circumstances now end up being a blessing in disguise.

---

[1] B. Goldberg. "Treating dental problems through past life therapy: A Case Report." *Journal of the Maryland State Dental Association* 1984, *27 (3)*, 137-139.

This event somehow stimulates tapping into your reserves of inner strength and you rise above the setback not unlike the Phoenix rising out of its own ashes.

There is a story I heard the comedian Buddy Hacket relate to Johnny Carson, when the latter hosted the *Tonight Show*. Buddy was a young comic working in a New Jersey nightclub during the 1950s. He played to a packed house every night. One night the club owner fired Buddy without giving him a reason. The club's attendance was still breaking records on the night of Buddy's dismissal. Years later while headlining in Atlantic City, Buddy noted his old boss sitting in the front row. He had the club invite this former employer to Buddy's dressing room after the show.

When Buddy Hacket asked his former boss why he fired him, the answer astounded him. This New Jersey club owner nicely informed Buddy that he knew Buddy was too good for his "joint." If he had not fired Buddy, he might very well have been still working there. We could all use the friendship and wisdom of Buddy Hacket's former boss.

The Effects Of Fear

The many emotional consequences of fear often result in mistakes. Fear can literally exhaust one in body and mind. It can render you incapable of effective action or thought.

Fear can add to an incapacity already present, or induce a new one entirely on its own. It can rob you of power and prevent you from acquiring power.

As far as the mind is concerned, fear commonly leads to confusion, indecision, loss of willpower, emotional shocks, poor concentration and faulty memory. It can drive a person to depend on illegal drugs and alcohol. Other effects include interfering with one's job, preventing one from embarking on new adventures, and causing all forms of mood swings from anxiety to depression.

Fear also exerts an effect on our physical body. It can cause disorders in our circulatory, respiratory and digestive systems. Fear may cause excessive sweating, sexual dysfunction (impotency and premature ejaculation in men and frigidity in women), headaches, loss of appetite and weight, profound exhaustion, speech defects, loss of muscle control, paralysis and psychosomatic pain. In short, fear can make you a slave to dysfunctional symptoms and behavior.

Hypnosis And Fear Removal

One way to remove a fear is through the use of hypnotic suggestion. Since your mind created the fear in the first place by accepting negative suggestions and programming from the outside world, why not reverse this process?

Your mind will respond to anything it receives, as long as the suggestion does not violate your moral or ethical code. Imagination and a suspension of your belief system are used to produce the effects of self-hypnosis. Refer back to chapter 4 and the basic self-hypnosis exercise. I did not create those relaxation feelings you felt; you did.

Every type of fear you can name owes its existence to imagination. We define imagination as the creative component of our mind. It is that faculty whereby we

₁₀duce mental pictures by visualizing forecasts of what the future holds, or, for that matter, pictures of what we feel the past held or the present is holding.

Here is a simple exercise you can do to use imagination to lessen your fears. Write the following message on a 3x5 index card:

> *When you read this message at bedtime, while holding this card in your hand, you will experience a natural tendency to drop this card. It will drop, and with the act of dropping this card goes the fears you currently possess. Soon you will free yourself of these former fears and now you will be able to function as the empowered person you were always meant to be.*

Practice reading this to yourself just before you retire for the evening. At first glance I know you think this method hasn't got a snowball's chance in hell of working. It won't take much of an effort to test this theory. One of my patients overcame a fear of abandonment she had for fifteen years, by using this technique.

You can try this exercise at any time during the day, but bedtime is the most efficient start. Just before retiring, your imagination is more easily aroused. You will use your imagination quite a bit during the REM (dream) cycle at night, which totals three hours.

When the card drops out of your hand, and it will, you will go to sleep more easily. Your mind now concedes that something has happened. If you can program your mind to drop the card, what other wonders can suggestion do? As insomnia is common with fearful people, the good night's rest alone is worth the effort.

Social Manifestations Of Fear

We live in a civilized society. It is rather difficult to custom design your own destiny if you are afraid of people. Like it or not, you must learn to get along with and be comfortable with all sorts of people if you expect to succeed in life.

Here are some examples of fear of the unknown involving other people:

- Avoiding social contact at a gathering because you fear that everyone else is smarter, more cosmopolitan, more skillful, more talented and so on. You refrain from participating in conversations and just observe others, being anxious all the while.
- You hang onto one person all evening at a party because you feel safe. It may be easy to relate to this individual, but your real motive is fear of being rejected by others.
- You are afraid to ask for help in your job or school because you don't want others to be aware of your ignorance on some minor point.
- Your social life consists of seeing the same people or couples over and over due to your fear of meeting new people.

The previous examples do result in certain dysfunctional payoffs:

- By removing the unknown from your life, you are keeping your fears of the unknown to a minimum. It is always "safer" to avoid the unknown. Unfortunately, growth is now impossible, and so is empowerment.
- You can rationalize your motives by saying it's the "right thing," or adult thing, to stay with the familiar. In reality it is an action determined by fear and insecurity.
- By keeping your life as routine as possible, you eliminate the need to think on your feet. All you need do is function by reflex and simply repeat past behavior patterns and responses.

Simple Strategies To Overcome The Fear Of The Unknown

- Decide now to take a risk on something relatively minor that may involve failure, but offers a significant reward.
- Try something within the next week that you have been avoiding for several years. Do not be concerned about whether you succeed at this task. Just do it.
- Purposely try something new. This could be ordering a different meal at your favorite restaurant, or buying a totally different outfit at your regular clothing store.
- Eliminate the fear of having to explain your actions for everything you do. Purposely do something that a family member, friend or business associate will comment on. Say to them, "I just felt like doing this, and I don't care to tell you why."

- Take an unplanned vacation (no maps or reservations). Talk with an acquaintance that you have purposely avoided because of fear of that person's reaction to you.
- Focus your awareness on something foreign to you as you are performing this task. Acknowledge the fact that you might not do this task correctly at first, but that is OK. The first step in mastering the unknown and removing its fear is awareness.
- Confront those people in your life whom you fear the most. Tell them you have feared them in the past and work out your differences, or simply enlist their assistance.

Fear of failure is most often the fear of someone else's disapproval or ridicule. If you let them have their own opinions, you can begin to evaluate your behavior in your own terms rather than theirs. You'll come to see that your abilities are simply different, not better or worse than others.

- Confront yourself with the fact that your fears are out of proportion to the reality of the possible consequences. Use the expression, "What's the worst thing that could happen to me?" to drive this point home.
- Invite a group of people to your home who are relative strangers and who represent a wide variety of viewpoints. Do not invite your usual clique of friends and keep this gathering as unpredictable as possible.

The entire process of overcoming fears begins with new beliefs, attitudes and changes in previous avoidance behaviors. This is followed by actively challenging old systems and people and moving on in new functional directions. Growth begins when you conquer fear.

Hope will now sprout, and you will develop a sense of personal power. Insomnia and other psychosomatic complaints will disappear, and the energy wasted on worrying thoughts will now be diverted to other channels and used to better effect. The thought, "I can and I will win through," instead of "I'll never pull through," will develop in you, and give you the strength to deal with the world you live in and lay a solid foundation for custom designing your own destiny.

Chapter 8
The Self-Image
Play Me Or Trade Me

By now you can see a steady progression in this book. We are laying the foundation for you to empower yourself and be in a much better position to custom design your own destiny. Understanding the difference between fate and destiny was established in chapter 2. Removing success myths and creating a formula for success followed in chapters 5 and 6, respectively.

Chapter 7 deals with overcoming fear and prepares you for building up your self-image. The self-image is the foundation that controls and affects your entire life and the way you respond to your universe. It is the key to human personality and human behavior. Change the self-image and you change the personality and the behavior.

The title of this chapter means quite simply that you use your self-image as is (play me) or change it (trade me). In other words, don't whine and complain about your misery, do something about it. Changing the self-image is exactly what you can and should do. In working with over 11,000 different patients since 1974, I have found that prior to completing their hypnotherapy, these patients did not have a self-image acceptable to themselves, nor were they at a level that would assure them of being able to custom design their own destiny.

Your self-image defines, for the moment, what you can and cannot do. It sets the boundaries of possible accomplishments. In order to broaden your horizons and expand your potential, you need to develop and enhance your self-image. This will now fill you with new talents, new abilities, new capabilities and the mechanism for transforming failure into success.

It is this concept of self-image that explains the differences in various personalities noted in psychosomatic medicine. For example, consider these personality types:

- Disease-prone
- Health-prone
- Unhappiness-prone
- Happiness-prone
- Codependent
- Empowered
- Failure-type
- Success-type
- Pessimistic
- Optimistic

The Self-Image
Play Me Or Trade Me

There is a saying in reference to the latter two personality types. A pessimist sees a glass half filled with water as half empty. The optimist looks upon this same glass as half full. I prefer the concept of realistic idealism, and always try to think that my cup "runneth over" (that is why there is room in the glass for more water).

It is critical to build up your self-image, since this is the way you view your world. We discussed how imagination affected the development and removal of fear in chapter 7. Our nervous system cannot tell the difference between an actual experience and an experience imagined vividly and in detail. Twentieth-century psychology has focused on the concept of the self-image and its improvement. It is, by far, the most significant contribution the behavioral sciences have made to our growth as individual souls. Although our self-image may be quite different from the more superficial projection of our conscious mind proper (defense mechanisms), it functions as a type of blueprint of our true selves.

Our self-image may be precise, vague, functional, dysfunctional, empowered, codependent and a myriad of other possibilities. It is a result of our beliefs, attitudes, fears and programming. This blueprint is not "etched in stone" and therein lies the beauty of this system. We can always change our blueprint and grow.

Although our self-image results from our interactions with other people and our environment, past experiences, our successes and failures, it will respond to reprogramming through self-hypnosis techniques. Once we compose a picture of our self, beliefs about this blueprint become real to us and we now act upon these beliefs as if they were hard facts.

Your behavior, feelings, actions, talents, fears and insecurities are always in accord with this self-image. This results in your acting like the type of person you perceive yourself to be.

By the principle of programming and creating your own reality, you manipulate the world around you to manifest this concept of yourself. Failure-type individuals will some way and somehow create situations in which they will fail. Others who are success-types would turn this very same opportunity into a positive conclusion.

The defense mechanisms play an important role in the failure-type by rationalizing any unsuccessful result. Expressions such as "I was meant to suffer," or "I guess I'm not worthy", surface to justify these situations. A vicious cycle of failure becomes established and accepted by you due to the repetition of this failure pattern. It becomes a Catch 22. By being passed over on a promotion for a position that you are most qualified for, you now utilize that failure as evidence that you weren't really qualified in the first place.

In social situations you can imagine a young woman desiring to talk to a certain man she is attracted to, but procrastinating this communication because of a fear of rejection. Her self-image is too low to initiate this contact. Later she observes this same man engaged in a conversation with another young woman possessing a higher self-image. As this leads to the development of a relationship between these two individuals, our original woman now accepts the belief (now a fact) that she just isn't good enough to meet Mr. Right. This can often result in her becoming involved in dysfunctional relationships with a series of Mr. Wrongs.

One of the best examples of this principle applies to salespeople. Salesmen and saleswomen are constantly tested by the public. Their attitude, behavior and self-image will determine their success at closing deals. Salespeople are only as good as their belief in themselves and their product.

Several years ago one of my elderly female patients related a story of how she helped her son improve his sales ability. This kindly woman could not get through to her son, who was exhibiting several SDSs and was depressed about his poor sales record.

His mother informed him of an old European remedy her mother had given her just prior to her death. Since the salesman had held his late grandmother in rather high esteem, he considered her an authority figure. He agreed to try this remedy and his mother proceeded to prepare it. She told her son that she would place a small amount of this cure in a bowl of chicken soup to disguise the taste. Upon consuming this soup the salesman appeared to beam with confidence.

During the next three months this man set all sorts of sales records with his company. His personal life improved and he felt and looked years younger. His mother confessed to me that all she did was give her son a bowl of ordinary chicken soup, laced with a white lie. I informed her that the soup she served was far from ordinary. It contained an elixir of confidence and stimulated her son's self-image growth allowing him to custom design his own destiny.

You are never too young or old to initiate this process of improving your self-image. This will result in alterations in your behavior, habits, personality and way of life. This is more than mere positive thinking. Positive thinking alone is like trying to use willpower (conscious mind proper) to eliminate a smoking habit. It may work for a while, but eventually you will substitute overeating or become very neurotic and resume the old smoking habit. The true origin of the difficulty is not removed by this method.

Once you fail at a particular task, the positive thinking becomes negative reinforcement of the still-existing belief that you are just fated to fail. The heart and soul of the problem is the self-image, with its beliefs, attitudes and programming. These must be changed and improved, not merely covered over with positive thinking.

Once you alter this concept of self-image by reprogramming it and improving its quality, all other aspects of your life consistent with this new self-image are accomplished easily and naturally. This principle has been established by thousands of studies and has been represented by the expression, "Whatever the mind can conceive and believe, it can achieve."

Prescott Lecky, in his book *Self-Consistency: A Theory of_Personality,*[1] was one of the pioneers in self-image psychology. According to Lecky, personality is composed

---

[1] P. Lecky, *Self-Consistency: A Theory of Personality* (New York: Shoe String Press, 1961).

of a system of ideas, which must be consistent with one another. Inconsistent ideas, he found, are not acted upon and are simply rejected. Only ideas which *seem* to be consistent with this system are accepted and incorporated into the self-image.

Lecky termed the "ego ideal" the foundation of the personality. This is the base upon which all other ideas were built. The ego ideal is the individual's self image. Being a teacher, it was simple to test his theory on several thousand students.

The hypothesis Lecky formulated stated that poor students perform below their potential because doing well academically would be inconsistent with their self-image. It had nothing to do with inherent intelligence. Lecky then designed various ways to assist his students in raising their own self-image. These students were counseled and trained to redefine themselves in a positive light. The results were nothing short of astounding. In one case a student had failed so many of his classes that he had to repeat the entire year. He had misspelled 55 words out of 100 just prior to entering Lecky's program. The following year this same student raised his general academic average to 91, and became one of the school's most accurate spellers. Another male student was dropped from one college due to poor academic performance, and through Lecky's assistance entered Columbia University and consistently made the dean's list.

Other examples cited by Lecky were a young male student who was informed by a testing bureau that his English scores were too low for him to consider college.

This lad, subsequent to entering Lecky's study, won an honorable mention the following year for a literary award. Another young female student failed Latin four times. She finally completed the next year with a B grade in this language.

How did Lecky work his magic? These students did not possess too low an IQ. They all had the potential for academic success but lacked the appropriate self-image. By identifying with their failures and mistakes, they considered themselves failures in general. This now programmed them to fail time after time.

By reprogramming their self-image, these students altered their ego ideal and began to think of themselves as successes. They now acted in a manner consistent with success and did far better in school as well as in other areas of their lives. This same technique was used by Lecky to assist these students in eliminating nail biting and other bad habits, even stuttering.

One secret of success is to attain a high level of fulfillment in life. In order to accomplish this, you must raise your self-image, and other factors in your life will then improve and become consistent with this new higher image of yourself. In chapter 12, I will present what I term the "New-You" technique. Lecky's work previously discussed provides a firm scientific foundation for this principle.

It is critical that your self-image be one that you can believe in and trust. You must be proud of the inner you, the real you. If you are ashamed of whom you are today, you will block creative and other facets of your being that could act to improve your self-image. This will make it impossible for you to be empowered and to custom design your own destiny.

Did you ever notice someone who is trying to convince you to buy something, or who tries to deflect your lack of satisfaction with a service they performed for you? They will appear nervous and unsure of their "pitch." It is not difficult to sense that they are attempting to fudge their viewpoint and con you. These "weasels" have a very low opinion of themselves and an even lower one of you. Their actions are quite consistent with their self-image. Do not use them as role models, but learn from these less than ethical people what not to do. Know yourself and take an objective inventory of both your strengths and weaknesses. Your self-image should be based on a realistic appraisal of who you are today. We will work on raising that image, but do not delude yourself. Get the facts and work on these deficiencies.

You will always feel good when your self-image is secure and intact. Anxiety will be experienced when this concept of self is threatened and insecurity dominates. By raising your self-image, you are now free to be yourself, a new you, and to express yourself in a positive and confident manner. You can now maximize your abilities and creative expression. The latter quality is quite necessary if you are to custom design your own destiny. The opposite situation may result in your becoming difficult to get along with and hostile.

What we really want is more life in our existence on this planet. By more life I am referring to success, happiness, peace of mind, fulfillment, a sense of worth and so on. We enjoy life more when these qualities are established.

The inability to establish these desirable qualities results in such things as self-hate, fear, anxiety and a host of other SDSs. This will result in a choking-off of life and condemn us to a life of misery and frustration.

You might wonder just what this mechanism is like that can literally turn our lives around and transform a failure-type into a success-type. I can unequivocally state that this is an impersonal mechanism that responds routinely to the positive programming I have alluded to throughout this book.

This system works automatically to assist you in achieving any goals of success and happiness, or unhappiness and failure. It all depends on how you program your subconscious. This is an impersonal system and negative programming will result in a failure-type personality. Positive programming gives rise to a success-type individual.

We will use imagination and the creation of mental images to attain these goals of building up the self-image. Your limits and range of accomplishments are controlled by your self-image. Whatever the mind can conceive and believe it can achieve. In chapter 12 we will also deal with reality and allow the future to communicate with us.

The data we feed into this mechanism in the form of beliefs, attitudes, thoughts and interpretations program our subconscious mind to act in accordance with this programming. By learning, experiencing and practicing new ways of imagining, remembering, thinking and acting, you will improve your self-image and custom design your own destiny.

Do not be concerned with your ability to visualize. It is true that this creative talent has degenerated with the advent of television. Your parents and grandparents most likely possessed higher levels of this visual ability. The quality of your visualizations is not critical to the successful application of these techniques. Just remember that visualization is no more difficult than the process of remembering some scene out of the past, or worrying about the future. Acting out new action patterns is no more difficult than making a decision to alter some previous behavior pattern (such as taking a different route to work or school) and carrying it out. You have now just created a new reality and have laid the groundwork for making other changes to your psyche.

Here are some helpful hints that will assist you in improving your self-confidence:

1. Use your creative abilities. Your visual imagery talents combined with your psychic awareness will unlock an energy flow that will result in your accomplishing goals. As you do this, you feel better about yourself and this leads to more confidence as you begin work on your next goal. You do create your reality. The world in which you live begins in your mind.

2. Practice discipline. It is impossible to attain any desirable goal without sticking to your plan. This conscientiousness is what I mean by discipline. Only people with self-confidence can be disciplined consistently. This

discipline will seem tedious at first, but as you improve your self-confidence, it will become ingrained.

3.   Replace your usual rational thought processes with an open and intuitive attitude. When you suspend rational thoughts (the defense mechanisms or ego), you are enhancing your creative and psychic talents. The last thing you want to encourage is left brain (rational) activity which will only push away any attempt at psychic development and improvement to your self-image.

4.   Assess the words you use in your everyday conversations with others. This also applies to what you say to yourself. Catch yourself when you say, "I am getting fat," or "I just can't seem to get anywhere." These words will program your subconscious and lower your self-confidence.

5.   End the natural tendency to doubt yourself. Doubts prevent growth. You cannot function as a self-confident soul by constantly doubting everything you do or say, or every decision you make. Eliminate the words, perhaps, maybe, I'll take that under advisement, or I can't make a decision. There are times when you will need to acquire more information to make a choice, but these will be the minority of situations you will face in your daily life.

An Exercise To Increase Your Self-Confidence

1.   Sit, relax and breathe deeply. Visualize yourself in your favorite relaxing environment. This may be the beach, a park or a cabin in the woods. Add the sounds of nature and the time of year you enjoy most.

2.   *Imagine yourself walking along in your favorite environment while looking up at the sky. You notice a rainbow has appeared and you focus your attention on the colors. You see red, orange, yellow, green, blue, purple and violet.*

3.   *As you stare at this rainbow, you realize that as long as you can see it you can accomplish anything you want to do. It is not necessary for this rainbow to be present for you to accomplish your goal, but its presence assures a successful attainment of any quest.*

4.   *Sit down now and think of the kind of person you would like to become. Review personality traits, health issues, finances and relationships. Focus on specific goals and aspects of your personality. Look up again and note the rainbow. You are now able to accomplish this goal of becoming who you want to be.*

5.   *Imagine a large television screen in front of you. Now project the ideal you on the right side of this large TV.*

6.   *This is called a split-screen effect as you now project an image of how you are on the left side of this TV. Imagine yourself now adjusting the fine-tuning knobs of this TV.*

7.   *As you adjust the TV the ideal image of you becomes crystal clear, while the current image of you goes out of focus and then disappears completely. The ideal you is your new reality.*

8.   *Look up one more time and note the presence of the rainbow. This image of you is now your new reality.*

9.   *Meditate on this image for at least five minutes with soothing New Age music playing in the background.*

10. Finally, breathe deeply, open up your eyes and say, "I am confident. I am in charge of my life and I now claim my power to improve my confidence level every day." End your trance as usual.

Improving The Learning Process

Another application of your empowerment will be to speed up the learning process. We learn better when we study in hypnotic levels. The right brain is far more efficient than the left brain. The following suggestions (applied after practicing the self-hypnosis exercise previously given) will help you to improve your learning ability through the application of your psychic subconscious mind's ability to be reprogrammed.

1. Give yourself positive statements about your intelligence and ability to learn.

2. Always use self-hypnosis exercises before doing any reading or other focused concentration activity.

3. Visualize yourself successfully attaining a goal. This might be an "A" on an exam, or some other desirable goal.

4. Ask your Higher Self for assistance in facilitating your learning.

5. Program yourself with the following statements when you are in a relaxed state:

      A. I am a good student and enjoy studying.

      B. I remember what I learn.

      C. My mind will give me any information I desire.

      D. Learning is fun and easy.

E. My subconscious allows me to learn
   faster.
F. My mind will always present information
   to me when I need it.

You can add to this list. I highly recommend making a
tape and playing it prior to any study periods.

Chapter 9
Getting Control Of Your Life

Taking control of your life requires you to eliminate factors that prevent growth. We have already discussed SDSs and fear, but two other emotions need to be presented. These are guilt and worry, two absolutely useless and potentially dangerous emotions.

Guilt

Guilt is the result of over-obsessing about mistakes made in the past. This results in a present immobilization of your thoughts and feelings over behavior that is past. You now tend to focus on a former event, feel dejected or angry about something you did or said, and use up your present moments being occupied with feelings concerning past attitudes.

When you feel guilty, what you are actually doing is reminding yourself that you've been a bad person because of something you said or didn't say, felt or didn't feel, did or didn't do. You respond by feeling bad in your present moment. You are brainwashed to believe that when you really care about anyone or anything, you show this concern by feeling guilty about the terrible things you've done, or by giving some visible evidence that you are concerned about someone's future. Do you really have to exhibit a neurosis to be considered a caring person?

I classify guilt as a useless and potentially dangerous emotion because you are feeling immobilized in the present over something that has already taken place and no amount of guilt can ever change history.

Growth is learning from your past and resolving not to repeat mistakes. This form of learning is a healthy and necessary component of our empowerment. When you are prevented from taking action now as a result of immobilization brought on by guilt, you are compromising any potential growth.

We use guilt to displace responsibility for our behavior from ourselves to others. This blame game ("You made me feel guilty.") is a no-win SDS. Winning the approval of others can be another pay-off for feeling guilty. Even though these individuals may not approve of your behavior, by feeling guilty you are showing that you know the proper way to behave and are making an attempt to fit in.

One last psychological reward for guilt is an attempt to win pity from others. Your priorities have shifted from earning acceptance and respect to one of having others feel sorry for you.

The above "dividends" of guilt represent a low self-image. Guilt is a choice, something that you exercise control over. If you don't like it and would prefer to make it go away so that you are entirely "guilt-free," here are some beginning strategies for eliminating guilt and placing yourself in a better position to custom design your own destiny:

- Objectively list the current things in your life that you have been avoiding due to guilt feelings about the past. You will facilitate the elimination of this guilt by working on these issues.

- Accept certain things about yourself that you've chosen but which others may dislike. Winning your own approval is the first step to depending on the acceptance of others.

- Assertively confront others in your life who attempt to manipulate you with guilt and inform them that you will no longer accept this behavior. You will find that the behavior of others will begin to change once they see that their previous effect upon you has vanished.

- Accept the fact that regardless of how disappointing a past event was, there is nothing you can do to change this circumstance. Feeling guilty about it will not change the past, nor make you a better person.

- Reconstruct your system of values to eliminate those that are impossible to achieve or are just plain superficial. Develop a new set of values and ethics that are more realistic and not imposed by others. Keep room in your value system for change and growth.
- Take a realistic look at the most common and strongest aspects of your life associated with guilt. Eliminate all of those useless and self-destructive attachments and apply the new value system you established in the previous step.

Worry

Worry is defined as being immobilized in the present as a result of things that you think are going or not going to happen in the future. Worry is the contrivance that keeps you immobilized in the now about something in the future – frequently something over which you have no control. Planning for a more desirable future is not worry. It is only when you exhibit this immobilization component that planning becomes worry.

There is absolutely no benefit to be gained by worrying. It will not ensure success and most certainly is not a characteristic of empowerment. Worry will create problems and add undue stress and anxiety to your life. By definition, most worry is about factors over which you have no control.

The following list encompasses what most of my patients appear to worry about:

- The economy.
- Health issues. This includes weight, smoking, heart attack fears, etc.
- Their job.
- The happiness of their spouse.
- The weather.
- Public speaking.
- Traveling.
- Their children and other family members.
- Security.
- Accidents.
- Paying bills.
- An afterlife.
- Flying.
- The death of parents, grandparents, etc.
- What others think.
- The car breaking down.

Worry brings with it certain psychological payoffs. Among these are the following:

- It prevents you from accomplishing activities and feeds into procrastination.
- This behavior enables you to avoid dealing with something uncomfortable currently in your life by immobilizing your thoughts, feelings and actions over something else in the future.

- Secondary gain and self-pity is fostered by the psychosomatic syndromes that can often be exhibited by this worry. Examples are cramps, headache, hypertension, backaches and ulcers.
- Worrying can be used to rationalize the fact that you are a caring person.
- This behavior can help you justify your SDSs. You can worry about what would happen if you eliminated these negative patterns. How would you handle empowered behavior? By avoiding changing, worry prevents you from seeing the truth about yourself.

Sample Exercises For Eliminating Worry

- *Illustrate the absurdity of your worry by asking yourself, "What's the worst thing that could happen to me and what is the likelihood of it occurring?"*
- *Reorganize your thought processes by viewing your present awareness as a time to live, not to obsess about the future. Initiate actions to accomplish your current goals. Action is the best way to eliminate worry.*
- *Today begin an activity that goes completely contrary to a current worry. Do something that is opposite to your behavior. For example, if you are continually late for work, arrive 30 minutes early. Surprise everyone, including yourself.*
- *Use productive thought and planning to eliminate your worry and to develop empowering behavior patterns.*

- *List all the things you have worried about during the past week, and see how your life has improved. When you prove to yourself that worry has neither accomplished anything positive nor assisted you in solving some problem, you have made a good start in the elimination of this useless emotion.*

As you may have observed, the key to the elimination of both guilt and worry centers on the present moment. Learn to live now and not waste your current moments in immobilizing thoughts about the past or future. Try this self-hypnosis script to achieve this goal. For this exercise use the first person "I" and "my" if you are recording your own tape. On my professionally recorded tapes I substitute "you" and "your." You can also do this if you are making a tape for someone else:

I am at peace with myself and my past. I forgive myself. I learn from the past and I release it. Every day, I feel better and better, all over, in every way. I am positive and my life becomes positive. I now see problems only as opportunities. I become positive and optimistic. I now develop clarity about my desires and goals. I evaluate the potentials and decide what I want. I now have the courage to make life-changing decisions. I now let go of all fears. I am self-assured and confident about my future. I draw joyous experiences into my life. I create a positive new life. I create my own reality, and I create a beautiful life. I release myself. I am free. I am confident and secure. I retain a calm, optimistic outlook.

I feel powerful and in control. My mind is calm and I think positive thoughts. I now accept the things I cannot change, and change the things I can. I create a happy, successful new reality. I am self-confident and self-reliant. I am worthy and deserving. I let go of the past, am responsible to the present, and create a positive new future.

I release my fears, and manifest my desires. I deserve love, prosperity and happiness. I mentally, emotionally and spiritually detach from all forms of negativity and negative people. From this moment on I will project a positive, loving, self-confident and empowered self-image that will permanently eliminate any previous guilt and worry from my awareness.

Mentally see yourself incorporating these suggestions into your new reality and functioning as a spiritually empowered soul.

Play New Age Music For 3 Minutes

1. Visualize yourself in your favorite relaxing environment. This may be the beach, a park or a cabin in the woods. Add the sounds of nature and the time of year you enjoy most.

2. Imagine yourself walking along in your favorite environment while looking up at the sky. You notice a rainbow has appeared and you focus your attention on the colors. You see red, orange, yellow, green, blue, purple and violet.

3.   As you stare at this rainbow, you realize that as long as you can see it you can accomplish anything you want to do. It is not necessary for this rainbow to be present for you to accomplish your goal, but its presence assures a successful attainment of any quest.

5.   Sit down now and think of the kind of person you would like to become, a person completely free from guilt and worry. Review personality traits, health issues, finances and relationships. Focus on specific goals and aspects of your personality. Look up again and note the rainbow. You are now able to accomplish this goal of becoming who you want to be. All of your guilt and worries have now disappeared. Do this now.

Play New Age Music For 4 Minutes
End your trance as usual.

Taking Control Of Your Weight

If I had to state the most common therapeutic issue I treat in my Los Angeles office, it would be weight control. Recent studies have shown that sixty percent of Americans are overweight and one-third of the population is obese (weight more than twenty percent of their recommended weight).

You will not project or represent an image of empowerment if you can't control your weight. Losing weight is really not difficult with self-hypnosis. In addition to being relatively simple, it's a lot of fun.

I'm sure I don't have to convince you of the problems encountered with being overweight. Obesity is a serious and unnecessary health hazard. It shortens your lifespan, interferes with your sex life and in today's society represents a red flag that you are not a happy camper.

Losing weight will assist you in taking control of your life because:

- It will change your personality by giving you greater self-confidence, a sense of pride, a feeling of accomplishment.
- It will make you less tired and sluggish.
- It will make you more popular with the opposite sex and improve your sex life.
- It will give you the inspiration to conquer other challenging problems.
- It will prolong your life.
- It will give you the added confidence to develop a better attitude toward other health issues.
- It will enable you to assist others in losing weight by you becoming an example of just what self can do.
- It will assist you in your quest to custom design your own reality.

Before I present specific scripts on using self-hypnosis to lose weight and maintain your ideal weight, here are some preliminary tips to facilitate your weight loss:

- Use the rapid self-hypnosis exercise to program motivation to lose weight. Make a firm decision to begin this program today.
- Reinforce all of the positive reasons why you want to lose weight. Add to my list and do this daily.
- Objectively assess your eating habits and look for obvious areas to change your diet.
- Globally assess your reasons for overeating. Are you frustrated with your job, sexually unfulfilled, or compensating for other unmet needs.
- Make a list of all the foods you routinely eat that are bad for you. Construct another list of foods that you like and are healthful and low in calories.
- Program yourself daily that you can and will maintain your ideal weight.

Here is a script for weight reduction using self-hypnosis. Use either the basic self-hypnosis exercise or the rapid self-hypnosis method prior to using these scripts. As I mentioned earlier, tapes work better:

> *Being overweight is unhealthful.*
> *You need your body to live.*
> *You owe your body this respect and protection.*
>
> *You have the power to reprogram your subconscious mind to reverse the prior thoughts of overeating and thinking of yourself as being overweight. You will, starting today, reprogram your subconscious to think of yourself as being thin and eating only the foods that are healthful and necessary for your body.*

You are going to lose all the weight that you desire to lose, and you are going to do this starting today. You will associate this relaxed state that you are now in with a relaxed attitude about losing weight. You will not need to count calories. As you lose weight you will gain more confidence and find further weight reduction easier. When you eat you will cut your food into small pieces and chew them slowly and completely before swallowing. Eat only one mouthful of food at a time. You will find that by eating slowly and smaller portions, you will enjoy your meals better and eat less food. You will find that halfway through a meal you will feel full. When this happens you will stop eating. You will never, never eat when you are not hungry.

Repeat these statements to yourself:

1. *I will get more filling satisfaction from less food every day.*
2. *I will eat slowly and only at mealtimes sparingly and properly.*
3. *I am losing weight steadily every week.*
4. *I am becoming slim and in better shape.*
5. *I have a stronger feeling every day that I am in complete control of my eating habits.*
6. *I am developing a greater liking every day for the foods that help keep me slim and in better shape.*

Remember, if you repeatedly deny satisfaction to a hunger pang, the desire eventually goes away.

From this moment on you will not think of yourself as being overweight. Every time such a thought comes into your mind, it programs your subconscious negatively. So you will now monitor your thoughts. Any thoughts or actions that come to your mind about your being overweight will be canceled out by your saying to yourself, "I am thin. I am thin." From this moment on you are only going to eat those foods that are necessary to keep you healthy and mentally alert. You are going to eat smaller portions of the foods necessary to keep you mentally alert and healthy. You will desire no more. You will be totally aware of eating - no longer eating by habit. From this moment on you will no longer eat between meals, or while watching TV, and you will have absolutely no desire to eat between meals or while watching TV.

You are going to set a realistic goal for your excess weight and you will carry it out successfully. Decide how many pounds you can realistically lose every week and you will lose this exact amount. Now repeat to yourself the realistic amount of weight that you can lose each week until you reach your ideal weight of _____ pounds.

You will find it easier and easier every day to stick to a reducing diet. You will enjoy smaller meals. The irritation and annoyances of everyday life are rolling off you like water off a duck's back. You will thoroughly enjoy the foods that are good for you.

You will gradually lose your craving for those, which will lead to the accumulation of fat and retention of fluids. Even when you cut out carbohydrate foods (including cakes and pastries), foods rich in starch, sweets, etc., there are still plenty of appetizing foods - salads, fruits, etc., which will begin to appeal to you more and more, as you eat more slowly. Thus you really enjoy the sight, smell and flavor. Consequently you will no longer be tempted into eating between meals and will have less and less difficulty in avoiding foods that are fattening.

You will exercise more each day and drink more water. As you gradually lose weight, you will become much healthier and fitter. Your personal appearance will improve.

Every day, your desire and determination to stick to your diet and change your former eating habits will increase to such an extent that it will completely overwhelm any temptation to depart from it. The temptation will eventually disappear. Some people fear being thin. But you don't have to fear losing weight. No matter why you gained the weight, for whatever reasons you became a compulsive eater, it is no longer important. What is important is that you have decided to change your eating habits, so that you can reach your desired goal - the image, shape, weight and size you desire. It doesn't really come into account whether you are fat or thin. You are still the same person. You still have the same power, the same personality, the same inner reality—no matter what your body shape, weight or size is. There is no need to fear losing any of your self when you lose weight. As the weight and inches roll off, as you control your eating habits, you remain the same you, only more trim. You do not need to fear that you are losing any of your protection. You are the same person. Don't wait until you lose all the weight to become the person you want to be, if you want to be someone different. Wear the clothes now that project your image. Sit, walk, and act with your thin personality. Don't worry about hiding the fat. Wearing fat clothes doesn't hide the fat. They only make you feel worse. So wear the clothes that you want to wear, that project the real you, now, as you are losing the weight. This will reinforce your desire to reach your goal.

As that extra weight begins to roll off, to melt away, to disappear, you are totally comfortable with your emerging fit and slender body. You are perfectly contented and at ease with the emerging slim, trim and slender you. You are in control of your eating habits. You are in control of your life. You are in control of losing weight and you are in control of your personality and your body. And you are perfectly happy with the inner you that remains as you lose weight and inches.

I truly believe that you are capable of dieting successfully and effortlessly to achieve and maintain your ideal weight of _____ pounds. You will be guided by the natural powers within you to achieve and maintain this healthy and attractive body.

Whenever you are tempted to eat fattening food or to violate any of these suggestions, you will automatically ask yourself if you really want to indulge. If you do want to, you will, but you will find that you prefer to exercise the hypnotic techniques and suggestions I have given you to reach and maintain your ideal weight.

Weight Reduction Visualization

Imagine yourself being at your ideal weight. See a friend/mate shopping with you. He/she is amazed at your thin appearance. Now visualize two tables in front of you. One table on the right has all the foods you like that add unwanted weight, list examples. Now draw a large red X through the table and imagine looking at yourself in a mirror (one that makes you appear very wide and short - like a carnival mirror).

The table on the left contains all the food that is healthful and will not add unwanted weight - fish, vegetables, eggs, lean meat, etc. Now draw a large yellow check through the table and imagine looking at yourself in a mirror (one that makes you appear tall and thin). Mentally tell yourself that you desire only the foods on the check-marked table. Imagine your friends, family, parents telling you how great you look by (specify a date) weighing only _____ pounds.

Visualize a photograph of yourself at your ideal weight.

Visualize a photograph of yourself at your present weight. Now focus on the photograph of yourself at your ideal weight. The other photograph disappears. Imagine how it will feel at your ideal weight of _____ pounds to bend over to tie your shoelace, walk, jog, wear a bathing suit on the beach. Now, mentally select an ideal diet that will help you reach your ideal weight of_____ pounds. Tell yourself that this is all the food your body will need or desire and it will <u>not</u> send hunger pangs for more.

One of the characteristics of failure that you are wise to avoid is frustration. Frustration brings with it excessive emotional feelings of deep dissatisfaction and futility. When frustration is chronic, it usually implies that your goals are unrealistic, or your self-image is too low, or both.

Frustration has a tendency to result in aggressive behavior. I recommend any type of physical exercise to dispel this aggression. The best channel of all for aggression is to use it up as it is intended to be used, in working toward some goal. Work remains one of the best therapies, and one of the best tranquilizers for a troubled spirit. Naturally, you are to continue with your self-hypnosis exercises to reprogram your subconscious while this is occurring.

Another aspect of your personality to eliminate on your road to success is resentment. Resentment is an attempt to eradicate a real or imagined injustice that occurred at some time in the past. This is no-win situation because you simply cannot change the past.

A vicious cycle now begins and you habitually feel that you are a victim of injustice; you begin to picture yourself in the role of a victimized person. You carry around an inner feeling looking for an external peg to hang itself on. It is then easy to see "evidence" of injustice, or fancy you have been wronged, in the most innocent remark or neutral circumstance. All this does is lead to self-pity and a lowered self-image.

It is your own response that causes this resentment. You can control it if you firmly convince yourself that resentment and self-pity are not ways to happiness and success, but ways to defeat and unhappiness. Remember, not everyone around you responded to this event with resentment.

If you allow resentment to dominate your emotions, you are incorporating an inappropriate belief that only impedes your ability to attain goals of success and happiness. The last thing you want to do is turn destiny into fate.

Take the word of someone who has accomplished many goals by applying the presented techniques; your life becomes worthwhile when you have worthwhile goals. When you are actively engaged in achieving goals, you become optimistic and this will improve your self-image dramatically. Others will quickly notice the new you.

Another helpful hint is to eliminate the tendency to confuse our "self" with our behavior. The fact that you did something does not characterize you as that type of person. For example, to say "I failed" (verb form) is but to recognize an error, and can help lead to future success. But to say, "I am a failure" (noun form) does not describe what you did, but what you think the mistake did to you. This does not contribute to learning, but tends to "fixate" the mistake and make it permanent. We seem to recognize that all children, in learning to walk, will occasionally fall. We say "He fell." or "He stumbled." We do not say "He is a faller." or "She is a stumbler."

The visual imagery exercise previously presented offered you the opportunity to succeed at little things in your life now. If we are habitually frustrated by failure, we are very apt to acquire habitual "feelings of failure" that color all new undertakings. But by arranging things so that we can succeed in little endeavors, we can build an atmosphere of success that will carry over into larger undertakings. We can gradually pursue more difficult tasks, and after succeeding in them, be in a position to try something even more challenging. Success is literally built upon success and there is much truth in the saying, "Nothing succeeds like success."

As an exercise I would like you to think of some success you have had in the past. It doesn't matter how long ago it took place or how small an achievement it was. The feeling of success you felt is more significant than the actual accomplishment. Take a few moments and use the rapid self-hypnosis exercise to relieve this successful experience.

As a follow-up exercise, keeping in this same frame of mind and preserving that success feeling, visualize a current or future project being accomplished and at its conclusion, emanating this same successful feeling you have now.

Chapter 10
Targeting Your Goals

In chapter 6 I detailed methods of formulating both short-term and long-term goals. Please review that chapter before practicing the exercises presented here.

We will now lay out efficient and simple techniques to assist you in targeting your goals. There comes a time in our quest to custom designing our own destiny during which a specific series of steps must be completed in order to attain a desirable goal.

Empowerment is the main principle here, as you will be documenting your game plan and creating your own reality simultaneously. By using a step-by-step approach, you are allowing yourself a more efficient and effective method to make your goals a reality.

The initial step deals with beliefs. We have at great length discussed both the importance of and the effect beliefs have on our behavior and attitude. On a two-column piece of paper list your inappropriate beliefs under a column titled Self-Defeating Beliefs. At the corresponding position in the right column construct a list of appropriate beliefs that replace those cited in the left column. This right column is labeled Empowerment Beliefs.

The nice thing about this system is that by just accurately preparing this list, you have undertaken the first step in transforming these self-defeating beliefs into empowerment beliefs. It should be pointed out that these lists we are discussing are a game plan, but not a rigid one. They function more as a guide, always subject to amendment.

The analogy of using a set of instructions to assemble a bookcase is relevant. The directions tell you what steps to take to reach your goal (a fully assembled bookcase), but you complete this at your own pace and can attain the final result by altering one or more of the steps. It is important to look upon these techniques as an enjoyable process.

Time Lines

To get a clear picture of your goals and the steps necessary to attain them, the best method I have used is what is termed a time line. The final goal is placed at the far right end of the line, and you work backwards from that goal to your current awareness. It is best to mark off certain necessary steps in increments along this time line with approximate dates, all subject to modification. Here is an illustration of a time line:

Targeting Your Goals

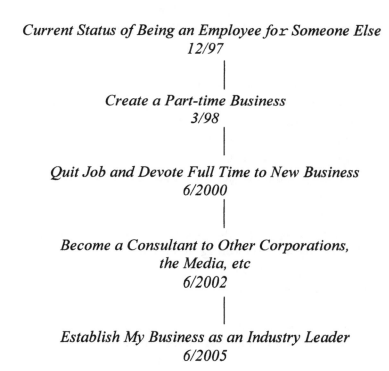

Current Status of Being an Employee for Someone Else
12/97

|

Create a Part-time Business
3/98

|

Quit Job and Devote Full Time to New Business
6/2000

|

Become a Consultant to Other Corporations,
the Media, etc
6/2002

|

Establish My Business as an Industry Leader
6/2005

You can see by the preceding time line that the complete transition from being an employee to a company to an industry leader in your own corporation is scheduled for completion within 7 1/2 years. The details concerning each step along the way can be treated as sub-goals.

For example, let us consider the March 1998, goal of creating a part-time business. This can be subdivided as follows:

Create a Part-Time Business

1. Review personal interests, professional abilities and formulate a potential business entity.

2. Conduct a market research in feasibility, competition, future trends, etc.

3. Develop a budget for creating this business.

4. Determine location for this entity - home based versus office building.

5. Take appropriate courses to learn more about establishing and marketing this business.

6. Design stationery, flyers, brochures, and organize an advertising campaign.

While you are completing and working on this sub-goal list, you may note one of your self-defeating beliefs surfacing. This is how you can integrate both lists. For example, let us assume that one of your inappropriate beliefs is that you are superior to others. In fact, you may even refer to other individuals as the "little people."

This form of arrogance and superiority complex will most certainly work against your contact with people. All businesses are people businesses. Trying to establish even a part-time entrepreneurial pursuit is not an easy chore. By projecting yourself with aura of "I'm better than you, so buy my product," you are laying the foundation for failure.

Confidence is great, and a high self-image is a necessary prerequisite for success. But overextending such a belief into arrogance will not help in your quest for success. You should never attempt a sub-goal unless you have changed the corresponding self-defeating belief.

The future you are constructing is you. It is designed and implemented by you. This does not imply a loss of creativity or a fixation of some type of script for the rest of your life. Always remember these goals have been decided on by you. You are custom designing your own destiny because you are creating it as you desire it to be.

The acts of writing down this game plan and constructing lists and time lines are very important for achieving your desired success. By not committing this plan to writing, you are symbolically placing your intentions to succeed in a non-priority, non-important category. This is the worst possible message to send your subconscious.

Think of other important actions you have taken in your life. When you bought a home or a car, graduated from school, paid your taxes, got married, joined the military, etc., did you not have some form of written documentation?

Your subconscious has long ago learned to identify written acknowledgments with priorities. By not writing down your goals, they become low priority and just another idea in the flotsam of your mind. To inform your subconscious of the importance of your game plan, write it down. Writing down these goals creates the necessary impetus for action and this will bring your desired success to fruition.

There are four levels of planning that facilitate you targeting your goals. These are:

- Beliefs List
- Time Line
- Sub-Goal List
- To Do List

In chapter 6 we discussed these to do lists and lifetime goal lists. The daily to do list will be your reassurance that you're serious about really reaching your goal. You will look at your list and know that everything on that list can be accomplished by you given your current abilities and priorities.

You may think of your time line and lifetime goal list as an accumulation of these to do lists. Whenever you consider the difficulty of attaining one of your long-term goals, you can focus on your daily lists and know that there are no difficulties you are incapable of handling. This leaves you free to fully enjoy the contemplation of your future success, unencumbered with doubt that your efforts towards custom designing your own destiny will be in vain.

Since you have written down your goals, your subconscious will prioritize them, and you will be many steps ahead of where you would be otherwise on your journey to becoming your empowered self.

We will now illustrate how to use the visualization techniques described in chapter 9 to bring about these desired results.

Using Visual Imagery To Target Your Goals

There are no limitations to the mind except those we acknowledge. Using visual imagery or mental movies to achieve success is not unknown throughout our history. Napoleon reportedly practiced being a soldier for many years prior to his military career. He imagined himself a commander and drew maps of the island of Corsica showing where he would place various defenses, making all his calculations with mathematical precision. Other notable examples of this form of mental rehearsal are Alexander the Great, Henry J. Kaiser and Conrad Hilton.

In order to use visualizations correctly, you must first clearly see a goal in your mind before you can complete it. When you do see a goal clearly in your mind, your creative success mechanism lodged within your subconscious takes over and does the job much better than you could do it by conscious effort or willpower.

This is more than mere positive thinking, as I explained before, because the subconscious reprogramming becomes a permanent part of your new success reality. Each of these exercises should be practiced with the hypnotic techniques previously given.

Let us illustrate this technique with a concrete example. Suppose you have an important job interview shortly, and want to do your best to land this position. Review in your mind the probable questions the interviewer will ask you and any tests you may be asked to take. Rehearse in your mind the answers to these questions and visualize a superior performance on any test. Now actually project in your mind yourself as an assertive, motivated and confident job applicant who is informed that he/she has the job. Concentrate on these positive images and reinforce this new high self-image and empowerment into your psyche.

This second illustration applies to abundance. By that I mean the acquisition of specific material gain. In this case your goal is to obtain legally a certain amount of money. First, set an exact amount of money in your mind that you desire. Now determine in your mind what service, time, effort, expertise or other aspect of your abilities you are willing to give in return for this specific sum. Set a date when you intend to receive this amount.

Next, devise a game plan for your desired goal and initiate this action immediately. Write out a clear, concise statement of the amount of money you intend to acquire; name the time limit for its acquisition; state what you intend to give in return for the money; describe clearly the plan through which you intend to accumulate it.

Twice each day, preferably upon arising and before retiring, read this statement and incorporate the belief into your mind that you already have this amount of money.

These visualizations are very powerful and can either assist or retard your progress. For example, if you picture yourself vividly as defeated, that alone will make victory impossible. Picture yourself vividly as winning and that alone will contribute immeasurably to success. Successful living starts with a picture, held in your imagination, of what you would like to do or be.

Your current self-image evolved out of negative programming and poor visualizations based on your experiences. We are using this exact natural technique to reverse this process and build up, rather than tear down, your image of yourself.

An easy way to incorporate this approach is by imagining yourself acting in a theater or on a movie screen. The important thing is to make these pictures as vivid and as detailed as you can. You want your mental pictures to approximate actual experience as much as possible. The way to do this is to pay attention to small details, sights, sounds, objects, in your imagined environment. You are creating a practice experience. And if the imagination is vivid enough and detailed enough, your imagination practice is equivalent to an actual experience, insofar as your subconscious is concerned.

When doing your own visual imagery exercises, see yourself acting, feeling, and "being," as you want to be. Do not say to yourself, "I am going to imagine this way tomorrow." Just say to yourself, "I am going to imagine myself acting in this way now." Imagine how you would feel if you were already the sort of personality you want to be. These techniques build a new image of self. After practicing it for a time, you will be surprised to find yourself 'acting differently,' more or less automatically and spontaneously 'without trying.'

Your current low self-image is the result of memories, real and imagined, you will have built into your subconscious mind. You will find it will work just as automatically upon positive thoughts and experiences as upon negative ones.

As an exercise use either the stage of a theatre or a movie screen and visualize yourself accomplishing each of these goals:

- A personal achievement - fulfilling relationship, losing weight, stopping smoking, making a new friend, etc.
- A professional success - a raise at work, a large sale, a promotion, establishing your own business.
- Resolving success - some past problem, whether personal or business.

To summarize these visual imagery techniques, you should on a daily basis:

- Visualize yourself in the future as you desire to be.
- Repeat this mental image and instill your ability to make this a reality.
- Practice encountering your desired reality by acting, in some manner, as if that reality were already fact.

Helpful Hints About Targeting Your Goals
And Creating Your Own Reality

People do not react to things as they are, but to their own beliefs and mental images. Consider the other person's feelings and viewpoints when you have difficulty with another individual. Success is a people business and to give the other person credit for being sincere but mistaken, rather than willful and malicious, can do much to smooth out human relations and bring about better understanding among people.

You must be open to seeing the truth about yourself and about life. More often than not, we do not like to admit to ourselves our errors, mistakes, shortcomings, or even admit we have been in the wrong. We do not like to acknowledge that a situation is other than we would like it to be. So we kid ourselves. And because we will not see the truth, we cannot act appropriately.

One secret to success is to ignore the temptation to see who is right, but to find out and implement what is right. It is desirable to admit your mistakes, but not to dwell on them. Make the appropriate correction and move forward with your life. Always be willing to make a mistake. Practice acting boldly with courage, both in your mind and in the outside world. Be sure that you are right and go straight toward that goal.

This voyage of self-discovery is a most exciting and challenging experience. Most of us have not entered this path with proficiency because of a lack of a clear goal and no understanding of the simple methods for creating this journey. To attain any spiritual goal, you must always know what it is you desire and how to realize it.

The techniques presented throughout this book instruct you on how to use your mind to create what you want for your life and to develop the personal power to sustain your growth over time. Unhealthy beliefs sabotage your natural ability to grow spiritually. Healthy core beliefs provide an ideal environment for this growth.

The following chart describes a healthy core belief system:

ASPECT OF LIFE	CORE BELIEF
Focused concentration	I have the ability to learn to clear my mind to facilitate attaining spiritual growth. I am able to get in touch with my feelings and freely express them.
Emotions	I am able to get in touch with my feelings and freely express them.
Relationships	I am able to be totally honest in all of my personal and professional relationships.
Empowerment	Take charge of my life and remove all victimizations I encounter.
My body	I care for and I nourish each of my physical needs.
Money	I create abundance using the principles of psychic empowerment.
Career	I maintain a healthy balance between my personal life and my professional goals.
Spiritual growth	Always access and listen to my Higher Self. All decisions and actions I undertake have a spiritual basis

In order to accomplish these goals, we must obtain information that gives us a clear purpose and goal of what we desire. Next, we need to formulate a vision of this goal and eliminate any limiting beliefs that stand in the way of this abundance goal. Finally, we use affirmations, visual imagery and reprogramming techniques to both access our Higher Self and effectively reprogram the subconscious with these goals in mind.

Remember that everyone is unique. Learn to develop appreciation toward your fellow human beings. Take the trouble to stop and think of the other person's feelings, viewpoints, desires and needs. Think more of what the other person wants, and how he or she must feel. The universe will reward you with a boomerang effect when you heed this principle.

Practice treating other people as if they had value, and surprisingly enough, your own self-esteem will increase. For real self-image is not derived from the great things you've done, the things you own, the mark you've made - but an appreciation of yourself for what you are. Get into the habit of remembering past successes and forgetting failures. What matters is the successful attempt, which should be remembered, reinforced, and dwelt upon.

Stop carrying around a mental picture of yourself as a defeated, worthless person. Stop dramatizing yourself as an object of pity and injustice. Use the practice exercises in this book to build up an empowered self-image. Place yourself in the position to target and accomplish your goals. Use errors and mistakes as a way to learning - then dismiss them from your mind.

When you change your self-image you are changing your own mental pictures, your own estimation, conception, and realization of that self. You really are better, wiser, stronger, and more competent now than you realize. Creating a better self-image does not create new abilities, talents, or powers; it releases and utilizes them.

Attracting Success

Here is a self-hypnosis exercise that promotes abundance:

Focus the power of your subconscious mind on attaining health, wealth and happiness. You are open and receptive to the good life. You know you deserve the very best that life has to offer. You can accomplish anything you set your mind to. You become more successful. There is no limit to your potential for success and excellence. You now take control of your life and create unlimited monetary abundance. You are now totally confident of your monetary success. You now focus your energy upon making more money, and use your imagination to create more wealth. You project power and confidence at all times. You are enthusiastic and willing to act. You are persistent, ambitious and determined. You make large amounts of money. You create great wealth. What your mind can imagine, you can create. You are self-reliant, self-confident, filled with independence and determination. You have great inner courage. You project a very positive self-image. You can do whatever you set your mind to. You see positive opportunities in everything you experience. Your positive thinking creates a positive life. You are confident you can do whatever you want to do. You are optimistic and enthusiastic. You are persistent, ambitious and determined. You create the space for satisfaction and happiness in your life, and do what you need to do. You accept what you cannot change and change what you can. You now choose to view your life as happy and satisfying. You have the self-discipline to accomplish your personal and professional goals. You direct your time and energy to manifest your desires. You are clear about your values and willing to commit to your goals. You know exactly what you want and you go after it, one step at a time. You have the self-discipline to do what you need to do. You fill your life with success, happiness and peace of mind. You are willing to spend the time and energy necessary to create wealth. You take complete control of your life. You are happy and fulfilled by your independence. Success becomes your way of life. You are self-directed and free. You are a self-confident winner. You feel good about yourself. You love and believe in yourself. You do things that make you proud of yourself. Your life now becomes a series of successes. You feel an intense inner drive to accomplish your goals. You free yourself from all limitations. You project power and confidence. Your lifestyle generates high energy. Mentally perceive yourself attracting success in all facets of your personal and professional life.

Play New Age Music For 4 Minutes

Now try this visualization:

Your goal is to obtain legally a certain amount of money. First set an exact amount of money in your mind that you desire.

Now determine in your mind what service, time, effort, expertise or other aspect of your abilities you are willing to give in return for this specific sum. Set a date when you intend to receive this amount.

Next, devise a game plan for your desired goal and initiate this action immediately. Write out a clear, concise statement of the amount of money you intend to acquire, name the time limit for its acquisition, state what you intend to give in return for the money, and describe clearly the plan through which you intend to accumulate it.

Now mentally incorporate the belief into your mind that you already have this amount of money. See yourself acting as if you have accomplished this goal.

Play New Age Music For 4 Minutes

End your trance as usual.

Characteristics Of Empowered People

Here are some characteristics of individuals who have mastered the art of empowerment. See how many of these traits you possess currently:

They never procrastinate.

They do not waste their time wishing that they had not done something.

They are doers, and are almost always engaged in work that will make other people's lives more pleasant or the universe a better place to live.

They can admit to making mistakes.

They are free from guilt and worry.

Any potential setback or problem is viewed as an obstacle to be overcome.

Business plans are constructed on a win-win-win basis.

They function on high energy, and are truly excited about everything they do.

They do not need to be loved by everyone.

They are not afraid to fail.

They do not blame others, they help others and themselves to assign responsibility where it belongs.

They are creative and encourage spiritual growth in others.

They are open to change and new paradigms.

They are never satisfied with the status quo.

They are healthy and always look younger than their chronological age.

Chapter 11
How To Design Your Future

In custom designing your own future you will be utilizing factors and forces outside the norm. The subconscious mind is still mostly a mystery to our scientists. This component of our consciousness is misunderstood, as reflected by the fact that current estimates state that we use less than 1 percent of our brain. I have not seen figures beyond 10 percent in the respected scientific literature for this percentage of brain use. I am not merely referring to the biological brain, but the entire range of consciousness. This includes the subconscious mind (alpha), conscious mind proper (beta) and the super-conscious or Higher Self (the perfect component of our alpha).

For our current purpose, let me simply state that we all have the capability to tap into a part of our awareness that will allow us to perceive our future and bring that data back to our current awareness. Although this may sound strange, the accomplishments of great inventors give credence to this concept.

Consider, for example, Leonardo Da Vinci. He designed models for the helicopter, submarine, tank and other wonders of the 20th century over 400 years ago! Thomas Edison conceded the fact that the source for his ideas (he received over 1,100 patents in his lifetime) originated from outside himself. He once refused to accept credit for an idea by saying that "Ideas are in the air." He went on to point out that if he had not discovered this idea, someone else eventually would have been its recipient.

The fact that we have access to ideas, facts, knowledge and memory other than from our own personal experiences has been proven scientifically throughout most of the 20th century through the work of Duke University's Parapsychology Laboratory, as well as many others. These institutions have shown that we have "psi," an extrasensory perception or ESP, such as clairvoyance, telepathy and precognition. Dr. J. B. Rhine of Duke University and others have found that there is a capacity for acquiring knowledge that transcends the five sensory functions. This extrasensory capacity can give us knowledge, certainly of objective and very likely of subjective states, knowledge of matter and most probably of minds. This also explains the creative inspiration, intuition and sudden revelation of artists, as well as scientists. For example, the composer Franz Schubert once informed a friend that from some undisclosed source he remembered melodies previously unknown to the world of music.

The mechanism you will be accessing in designing your future is characterized by certain principles that I have observed since my work in this field dating back to 1974. These principles are:

- The subconscious, when analyzing information concerning your future, treats this data as already occurring. You must have a specific goal either in actual or potential form and an end result.

- Your subconscious will function to help you manifest this goal that may already be in existence, or "discover" something that will lead you to create this goal in the near future.

- The subconscious will be positively programmed by remembering only successful results and forgetting (emotionally) the past setbacks. You want to learn what not to do by a review of these "failures," just don't get hung up on them.

- Your Higher Self and your subconscious mind work together - spontaneously, according to present need. This Higher Self will manifest itself more frequently when acting as if it is already there.

Using Visualizations To Prepare For Your Future Success

Changing beliefs is an absolute prerequisite to custom designing your future. It represents the foundation, along with the accompanying Higher Self-image, with which you are building this new destiny. To accomplish this, three techniques will be applied.

The first two are affirmation repetition, and act as if these changes (successes) have already occurred. Since the effects of these three techniques are cumulative, it is important to practice them daily. Get into the habit of using the exercises on a daily basis.

In the beginning of your trials with these methods, you likely will experience inappropriate beliefs. The exercises presented in this chapter, along with the previous chapters, will assist you in overcoming this temporary obstacle. These inappropriate beliefs become part of your defense mechanisms, and those beta entities do not relish the concept of being set aside.

One reason why you will succeed with properly applying these exercises is that you are doing something very few people even attempt. You are defining your goals and perceiving yourself as already attaining these rewards. This places you far ahead in the game of custom designing your own destiny.

The first technique consists of repeating affirmations. This needs to be done in a positive manner. For example, instead of saying "I won't fail and wind up in bankruptcy court," a better phrasing would be, "I am succeeding at this _____ goal and will be rewarded by earning _____ dollars by this specific date _____."

It is important that the first part of your affirmation be stated in the present tense, as in my previous example. This is done to reinforce the concept that you are "acting as if" it is part of your present reality. In addition, your subconscious does not distinguish between past, present and future as readily as your conscious mind proper. As we shall explore in chapter 14, the subconscious is immersed in the space-time continuum in which all time exists simultaneously.

If you state that you will be successful, you are programming your subconscious to perceive yourself as not successful now. This will lead to inappropriate beliefs that you are a failure, and consequently lower your self-image.

Your subconscious can only affect your current reality by its programming. It does no good to instruct it to change at some future date. It most certainly cannot undo past issues. The significance of committing these affirmations to writing in the form of goal statements has previously been discussed.

It is always wise to make your own tapes. You can always purchase professionally recorded tapes, as I mentioned before. For affirmations or goal statements you do not need tapes, as they are relatively brief.

Do not be concerned with meeting each and every future goal by the specified date. Many of these projected dates are simply educated guesses. The process is far more important than the completion date. You will always be guided by your Higher Self and by your subconscious as you continue on with your journey of empowerment.

All during this time you are improving your self-image. You will find yourself becoming aware of self-knowledge not previously known. In addition, you are now reducing both the potency and quantity of SDSs and preparing the foundation for this customized future.

One of your immediate goals is to disregard and eliminate inappropriate beliefs and replace them with the empowered ones. This will prevent you from entering into personal and professional relationships that repeat past patterns of you being victimized, frustrated and depressed.

Since you alone are in control of establishing (by reprogramming the subconscious) your new and positive self-image, you are in control of your destiny. By raising the quality of your own self-image, you will attract equally empowered people into your life that will assist you in your projects and make your future experiences more fulfilling.

Circumstances will now arise that may appear at first to be setbacks, but in the long run will educate you and challenge you to be the best you can be. The lessons learned and difficulties encountered will function as stepping-stones to your eventual success.

One nice thing about this approach is that while you are designing your own future, you are also fitting into a more universal game plan. This larger framework encompasses the futures of those you know now and will shortly meet. These other souls will assist you in achieving your goals and designing your future, and you will reciprocate with them and their respective destinies. Refer back to the Ed Morrell case I presented in chapter 2.

This method of creating a custom-designed future works because the strategy is tailored to you, by you, and for you. Who else but you could better define a series of steps best suited to your particular purposes? Your own role in creating this future further adds to your motivation, self-image and prognosis.

You are the *only* one who can precisely design the missing parts of the puzzle. Therefore the complete picture of your success is brought into reality. This could never be done as effectively by an outside source. In addition, this becomes a part of your own empowerment.

Wouldn't it be nice to look upon the future as one you had a hand in designing? By following these recommendations you need not fear tomorrow but instead welcome it with open arms. Applying the "New-You" concept we will discuss in chapter 12 means that no new activities will ever appear before you; they have all been accomplished by you already. Thus, you need not fear any task because you have, in a very real sense, already successfully performed the activity.

This destiny you are designing is a creation of yourself in the future by you. It is the ultimate example of empowerment. Let us not fall into the trap of writing-off this technique to wishful thinking. I present case histories in chapters 12 and 17 documenting the accuracy of this technique. Please refer back to chapter 1 for my own example.

When you practice with the visualizations, (the third method for changing beliefs) do your best to identify with the entire spectrum of conditions. Mentally see yourself in this personally designed future. Feel the emotions and be open to any sensory experience that accompanies the data and images.

The importance of affirmations revolves around the concept of past negative programming. This is because your family, friends, teachers and others may have said things to you or treated you in a way that resulted in a lowering of your self-image. Positive affirmations function to reprogram the subconscious to eliminate this baggage and free you to "be all you can be."

The advantage of acting as if your future goal has been accomplished sends an important success message to your subconscious. Now more and more opportunities will present themselves to you because you are more open to receive them and are sending out the appropriate signal (alpha) to attract the positive options into your life. This further changes your inappropriate beliefs to empowering ones and adds to your self-confidence and self-image. A geometric growth pattern now emerges, and you have just initiated the necessary steps toward creating your reality by designing your future. All this is accomplished with pre-knowledge of the future outcome of your goals.

Studies confirm the fact that your brain cannot distinguish between a real experience and one that is imagined. When you design your future by the self-hypnosis techniques presented in chapter 12, your body and mind actually accept the fact that this is the "new you." All of the requisite steps relayed to you by your subconscious are reality based. You need not worry about what to do next or if you are applying them correctly. It is simply a matter of readjusting your focus. Readjust from the ultimate goal, the ultimate future, to the first step. The entire game plan will be laid out before you and each specific step simply falls into place.

In summary, the following represent advantages to using this method and the "New-You" technique to your ultimate goal of custom designing your own destiny:

- Your confidence in general will increase, as you find yourself no longer worrying about the outcome of events in your life.
- You will receive information and ideas that you could not obtain from your conscious mind proper (beta).
- The little successes you initially have increase your motivation for additional applications of this technique, and further add to your self-image.
- A feeling of importance is felt, as you now begin to structure your life with specific steps and a timetable. This also means you are assigning an importance to the project of achieving the success and self-fulfillment that you desire.

Using the ideas set forth in this book will assist you in being much more connected to the universe, and allow you to experience more intimately the "inherent rightness" of your true desires for self-fulfillment. This will result in your placing the values on your life and your goals that should rightly be there.

Here are some additional tips to assist you in creating abundance:

1.   Accept the concept that you have the natural ability to create abundance. This goes back to the self-image issue that I have mentioned several times before. You must believe in yourself and that what you are doing is right. It is important to eliminate the "out there" form of thinking of abundance and bring it "in here."

By asking your Higher Self for assistance, you can rely on the fact that your abundance will improve only if it is meant to do so. Your Higher Self produces prosperity. It is not an isolated event.

2.   Select a higher value over a lower one. This does not suggest that you become obsessed with money or the prices of objects. There is a principle I call "realistic idealism." This means you pick and choose your goals. Sometimes there will be no material gain associated with this endeavor. By eliminating clutter and petty materialistic concerns, you can now free your Higher Self to help you with the big picture.

3.   Accept the fact that your mind has all the information and techniques available to create this abundance for you. When you use self-hypnosis daily, you are tapping into your Higher Self. This perfect, all-knowledgeable aspect of you will patiently teach you ethically how to attain your materialistic goals.

4.   Accept the unusual and expect the unexpected. There are no boundaries or limitations to what your mind can create and accomplish. Prosperity has a way of arriving when you least expect it.

5.   Do not attempt frivolous goals with these methods. You will fail repeatedly if you do. If you need a job,

visualizing one is not enough. You will still have to go out and look for one and face several rejections before you land the job you desire.

Always request assistance from your Higher Self. I have already presented several exercises on how to impress a job interviewer. Use these visual imagery techniques daily.

You can meditate on a specific job, a career change, or anything else that will facilitate attaining your abundance goals. Always keep your motives pure. It is not selfish to seek money and possessions. It is only selfish if you do it at someone else's expense or to get back at another person. If this is your goal, you may succeed in the short run, but you will hurt yourself in the long run.

Here is a simple exercise you can practice to help you discover your life's work:

*1.	Practice using the rapid self-hypnosis exercise first. Mentally stand in front of a chalkboard and gently request your Higher Self to list your current talents and abilities.*

*2.	Now list the types of jobs you have held in the past. Finally, list the job or profession you would like to enter or obtain.*

*3.	Meditate on these lists for five minutes. Now turn the chalkboard over and the answer to your question of a career choice will appear.*

Practice this exercise several times until you receive an answer.

Chapter 12
Applying The "New-You" Technique

Precognition

Can we really get a glimpse of our future and bring that knowledge back to our current awareness to assist our growth? The whole basis of the "New-You" technique using age progression with hypnosis relies on this very concept. Fortunately, the answer is yes, and I will present a hard science support for this from the field of quantum physics (the new physics).

Documented Cases Of Precognition

Before I discuss the theory of just how this technique works, here are some examples of documented cases of seeing into the future, otherwise referred to as precognition.

Mark Twain

When Samuel Clemens was twenty-three, (he had not yet adopted the pen name of Mark Twain), he worked as an apprentice pilot on the Mississippi steamboat *Pennsylvania*. His twenty-year-old brother Henry worked on another ship as a clerk. One night Sam had a vivid dream vision of a metal coffin in which Henry was laid to rest. Shortly after this precognitive dream, Sam received word that his brother had been killed and laid out just as Sam had dreamt. Mark Twain recalled this incident many years later to his biographer Albert Paine.

Foreknowledge Of A Plane Crash

In October of 1967, Mrs. Helen Peters of New Jersey frantically called the New York office of British European Airways (BEA) to inform them that their flight carrying her husband was about to crash. The BEA employee tried to assure Mrs. Peters that her worries had no basis and that her husband would be fine. The BEA plane crashed off the coast of Cyprus in the Mediterranean, killing all 66 passengers and the entire crew.

The Sinking Of The Titanic

Morgan Robertson wrote a novel in 1898 titled *Futility* in which a supposedly unsinkable ocean liner struck an iceberg on its maiden voyage and sank, carrying the elite society of two continents to their deaths.

Fourteen years later, in 1912, a similar "unsinkable" liner sailed from England with 3,000 passengers aboard. Like Robertson's craft, it was 800 feet long and weighed 70,000 tons but with far too few lifeboats. The real boat, like Robertson's, struck an iceberg and sank with the loss of more than a thousand lives. Robertson had named his boat the *Titan*. The real ship was the *Titanic*.

Socrates

Socrates (469-399 B.C.) had a highly developed sense of precognition. Once, out on a stroll with a group of friends, he elected to take a quite different and unaccountable course from the rest and urged his friends to follow him. Most of them saw no reason to follow him on this changed route and went their chosen way. Those who ignored his advice were seriously injured by a rampaging herd of wild boars.

Once Socrates turned to a friend and told him not to proceed with a secret project he had in mind. The friend looked curiously at Socrates, for he had neither hinted at nor confided his secret project. Socrates' friend was in fact planning an assassination but had at that stage told no one, nor were there circumstances or a past record of behavior from which such an inference could be drawn. The friend, regrettably, ignored the advice, proceeded with his plans, carried out the assassination, and was in due course arrested, tried and executed.

Jules Verne

This science fiction novelist is well known for his futuristic visions in such books as *From the Earth to the Moon, Journey to the Center of the Earth*, and *20,000 Leagues Under the Sea*. What is not common knowledge is that one of his most accurate works was rejected in 1863 by his publisher, Pierre Herzel. This novel was titled *Paris in the 20th Century* and depicted life during the 1960s.

Here are some of the technological references Verne makes in *Paris in the 20th Century*:

- electronic bank alarms
- subway transportation
- personal computers
- 24-hour convenience stores
- schools of the future in which audio and video equipment present information

Precognition is awareness of facts and circumstances in the future that cannot be accounted for by science or logic. Anything that can be explained in terms of subconscious knowledge, or by interpreting a known past sequence of events, or by an intelligent assessment of the situation based upon detailed information, cannot rank as precognition.

Precognition, in the sense in which we have been considering it, implies a human consciousness and is something experienced during a human lifetime. Both precognition and age regression imply that our conceptions of time are either fallacious or woefully incomplete, or both.

The problem presented by precognition is that the effect appears to precede the cause, violating causality laws of conventional physics. Since space and time do not exist independently but as a continuum known as space-time, this fourth dimensional paradigm allows an effect to come before a cause. Our brain is constructed to deal with only three dimensions (length, width and depth). This fourth dimension known as time (in reality the fourth dimension of the space-time continuum) often confuses our three-dimensionally oriented brain.

Professor John Taylor of King's College, London, had moved toward acknowledging the possibility of precognition, a phenomenon he once discounted. His hypothesis was that perhaps the brain emits *tachyons,* impulses traveling faster than light, thereby reaching into the future and then being reflected back to the brain, giving foreknowledge.

Professor Taylor's hypothesis about tachyons voyaging into and perceiving the future and returning to record it, was to some degree anticipated by those who marveled at the nature of human cells. It could be argued, that to some degree at least, cells have some type of built-in intelligence. There are billions of them in the human body, and the immense network of nerve cells in particular may constitute some mysterious transmitting and receiving system. If some form of energy is transmitted from the human body capable of traveling faster than light, it might not emanate from the brain itself. Nor, having traveled faster than light, and so into the future, would the impressions and messages necessarily be received directly by the brain. The brain might pick up the impulses after the outgoing energy waves had been reflected back, radar fashion, to the bodily source of transmission. Quantum physics clearly demonstrates that any tachyon would move in reverse time sequences.

We all possess a dormant capacity to have precognitions. They occur to us nightly in our dreams, we just don't remember them, except on rare occasions. Some people experience gazing or dissociative states during which they receive information about the future. I discuss this more fully in my book, *Astral Voyages*.[1]

Cleansing

The subconscious mind's energy is qualitatively lower than it should be. In order to raise this energy, I developed a technique back in 1977 called the superconscious mind tap. This technique consists of introducing the patient's

---

[1] B. Goldberg, *Astral Voyages: Mastering the Art of Soul Travel* (St. Paul: Llewellyn, 1999).

subconscious mind to its perfect counterpart (the superconscious mind or Higher Self).

When this is complete, the perfect energy of the superconscious mind assists in raising the energy of the subconscious mind by this exposure. Think of going outside your home on a chilly morning to get the paper. You may not be dressed as warmly as you could be, so you are cold. The moment you return to your nicely heated home, your body warms up. This is basic physics.

The soul's energy can never be lowered, but it can be raised. Conducting a super-conscious mind tap (or "cleansing") is the most efficient method I know of to boost the energy of the subconscious. Clinically this will be observed as an increase in self-image, motivation, energy and the expression of a success-type personality.

One of the most important aspects of cleansing is that 98 percent of this form of energy raising takes place in the dream or REM cycle at night. Your defense mechanisms do not function during this time, so there is nothing to prevent our soul's energy from raising its quality. There is no other time during the day when this situation exists.

Sleep laboratory research has confirmed the fact that we spend about three hours every night in REM sleep. Emotional cleansing occurs during this time; if not for this fact we would die of a heart attack from the cumulative effects of stress.

Energy cleansing does not happen automatically, since it is not required to preserve life. If properly trained, we use about one of our three hours in REM for energy cleansing. Since each minute in hypnosis is equivalent to three to four earth minutes, three to four hours of therapeutic energy cleansing is actually experienced by the individual. It is no wonder that this therapy is so short, successful and popular. The patient is trained in a relatively few number of sessions to be totally independent of the therapist and to attain any goal that is humanly possible. Superconscious mind tapes are given to the patients to assist them in this goal.

Another principle to consider is the fact that this energy cleansing brings about an emotional cleansing, which in turn affects a physical cleansing. The true cause of any issue is an energy block, so a superconscious mind tap effectively eliminates the true cause of any issue.

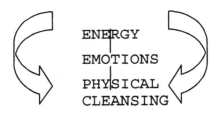

ENERGY
EMOTIONS
PHYSICAL
CLEANSING

You will note that the arrows always move down from the energy level to the physical state. Occasionally, the superconscious mind can bring about a physical release directly, as in the case of a headache.

Cleansing techniques can be done at light, medium or deep trance levels. Visual imagery is not necessary or even desirable when cleansing is initiated. In order to prevent the defense mechanisms from interfering with this cleansing during one of my sessions, I use a subliminal technique. I speak to the patient in a voice below that of very relaxing metaphysical music playing in the background.

Try this script to experience my superconscious mind tap:

Now listen very carefully. I want you to imagine a bright white light coming down from above and entering the top of your head, filling your entire body. See it, feel it, and it becomes reality. Now imagine an aura of pure white light emanating from your heart region, again surrounding your entire body, protecting you. See it, feel it, and it becomes reality. Now only your Higher Self and highly evolved loving entities that mean you well will be able to influence you during this or any other hypnotic session. You are totally protected by this aura of pure white light.

In a few moments, I am going to count from 1 to 20. As I do so you will feel yourself rising up to the superconscious mind level where you will be able to receive information from your Higher Self. Number 1- rising up. 2, 3, 4 - rising higher. 5, 6, 7 - letting information flow. 8, 9, 10 - you are halfway there. 11, 12, 13 - feel yourself rising even higher. 14, 15, 16 - almost there. 17, 18, 19 - number 20. You are there. Take a moment and orient yourself to the superconscious mind level.

Play New Age Music For 1 Minute

You may now ask yourself questions about any past, present, or future life issue. Or, you may contact any of your guides or departed loved ones from this level. You may explore your relationship with any person. Remember, your superconscious mind level is all-knowledgeable and has access to your Akashic records.

Now slowly and carefully state your desire for information or an experience and let this superconscious mind level work for you.

Play New Age Music For 8 Minutes

You have done very well. Now I want you to further open up the channels of communication by removing any obstacles and allowing yourself to receive information and experiences that will directly apply to and help better your present lifetime.

Allow yourself to receive more advanced and more specific information from your Higher Self and masters and guides to raise your frequency and improve your karmic sub-cycle. Do this now.

Applying The "New-You" Technique

Play New Age Music For 8 Minutes

All right now. Sleep now and rest. You did very, very well. Listen very carefully. I'm going to count forward now from 1 to 5. When I reach the count of 5 you will be back in the present, you will be able to remember everything you experienced and re-experienced. You will feel very relaxed, refreshed, and you'll be able to do whatever you have planned for the rest of the day or evening. You will feel very positive about what you've just experienced and very motivated about your confidence and ability to play this tape again to experience your Higher Self. All right now. 1, very, very deep; 2, you're getting a little bit lighter; 3, you're getting much, much lighter; 4, very, very light; 5, awaken - wide awake and refreshed.

It is not necessary to use subliminals on tapes, as studies show that they are no more effective than non-subliminal hypnotic tapes. During a session I can personalize the training instructions so that they are always relevant. This is why subliminals work well in person, but not on tape. Now let us discuss the concept of actually viewing your future.

Age Progression

The concept of going forward in time is called age progression. I prefer this term to precognition because the latter implies a mystical and unpredictable, ethereal experience.

By further enlisting the aid of the Higher Self through cleansing techniques, you raise your self-image permanently, and this "new you" now contains a set of beliefs that fosters karmic capitalism. You are never too young or old to initiate this process.

A technique I developed several years ago that I refer to as *spiritual restructuring* will enable you to easily apply self-hypnosis exercises. Here is a sample exercise that is easy to practice and incorporates the basis of this spiritual restructuring.

> 1.   *Prepare a list of beliefs and/or behavioral patterns that you would like to change or remove from your awareness. Always maintain a positive approach, so that you list these items in terms of what you would like, rather than what you don't want. An example would be "I am becoming more motivated and organized" is much preferable to "I don't want to procrastinate and fall behind in my work."*
>
> 2.   *Add to your list the situations or times of the day when dysfunctional behaviors or beliefs were exhibited.*

3. Now list the advantages of making permanent changes by eliminating these previous beliefs or behaviors.

4. Access your Higher Self by practicing the superconscious mind tap exercises. During one of the open spaces in the script ask your Higher Self to show you specifically how to permanently alter these beliefs, or eliminate the negative behaviors. Reinforce your ability to successfully apply this method by saying to yourself "I am ready, willing and able to initiate cleansing."

5. While still in trance, direct your focus on the future. Ask your Higher Self to guide you to a future date in which your goals are accomplished. Perceive yourself functioning as an empowered person at this time.

6. Stay in this trance for as long as you like and open your eyes to resume normal conscious mind functioning.

Throughout my career as a hypnotherapist I have emphasized two main paradigms. The first one is that we tend to initiate a form of self-defeating sequence whenever a desirable situation presents itself, and our self-image is too low. Second, psychic empowerment is the most important lesson our soul needs to learn during its sojourn on the physical plane. Fear is the main antagonist to psychic empowerment and spiritual growth. If you don't attain abundance, or any other goal, it is because you don't feel worthy of this goal, or you fear it. Spiritual principles teach us that we cannot make permanent changes in our behavior and thought processes until we have actually become the person we want to be.

Consider the goal to become financially independent. Now add to this a problem with compulsive spending. Unless you become the person who has overcome compulsive spending, you will never permanently establish yourself as a financially independent karmic capitalist. You may earn significant amounts of money, but you will spend more than you earn and have to earn it all over again. You simply can't win that way.

Age progression is simply moving in the opposite direction from age regression (going backward in time).

Before you write off age progression as wishful thinking, consider the fact that my patients have reported information from the future that they could not possibly control. Whether reading a newspaper headline about a future disaster, correctly obtaining a winning lottery number or ball game score, or a corporate merger of some Fortune 500 company, these events cannot be adequately explained by any other means.

Here is a simple illustration of the space-time continuum, which states that all past, present and future events are occurring simultaneously. This is taken from my book, *Soul Healing*:

> Suppose, for example, that you are in a helicopter above a major highway. You look down and see that traffic is stopped because of an accident. At this time you could radio someone in a car five miles behind the scene of the accident and

inform the driver of the upcoming traffic problem. Since you are in a helicopter above the traffic flow, you are actually detached from the scene itself. The driver that you are warning is immersed within the flow of traffic. In a sense you are reading the future of this car. If the driver of that car keeps driving on that highway, he will encounter the congested traffic that you are now observing. The helicopter represents another dimensional plane, and on a different plane there is no time as we here on Earth, (or on the highway, in this analogy), know it.

To extend the analogy further, note that from the vantage point of the helicopter you could also see what the traffic flow is like behind the car to whose driver you are talking. This would represent the past. The traffic ahead of the driver represents the future, and the traffic that the driver is experiencing now represents the present. You are, in effect, reading the past, present, and future from the helicopter. By leaving the Earth plane or entering into hypnotic trance, you can read the past or future without the restrictions that occur in the waking, or beta, state.[2]

Using hypnotic age progression to view your future is well within the paradigms established by quantum physics. We will discuss those shortly. For our current purpose, this marvelous technique can be applied to viewing the

---

[2] B. Goldberg, *Soul Healing*, op cit. p. 112.

potential outcome of a new job, relationship, investment or geographical move. There are endless uses to this method.

Before we go on to more advanced concepts, let me deal with the issue of "forbidden knowledge." Many of my patients and medical colleagues express concern that I may be violating some universal law by conducting hypnotic age progressions.

If patients or tape listeners were not supposed to receive information about their future, my method simply would not work. Your Higher Self is the censor in this case. When you are ready to receive this data it allows you to access it. If you are not prepared for this information, there is nothing short of consciousness expansion (see chapter 14) that will permit any of this data to "get past the goalie." There is an old saying in metaphysics, "When the student is ready, the teacher will be there."

Frequencies

According to quantum physicists, there is not just one future, but an unlimited number of parallel universes or frequencies. My twenty-two years of experience in conducting progressions shows that there are five main paths or frequencies. One of the many advantages of using progression hypnotherapy is to be able to lay out these five paths and choose your ideal path. This ideal frequency will then become your new reality.

Your ideal frequency out of these five options never changes. What you are accomplishing by cleansing is improving the quality of each of these frequencies. This has the advantages of:

- Immediately improving your current path, thus allowing you to receive instant positive feedback.
- Maximizing the potential of all of the five frequencies so that each of them will be improved. This also results in your ideal frequency being even more fulfilling.

Let us assume that out of your five possible major frequencies number 4 represents your ideal path. If you did not undergo cleansing, frequency 4 would still be your ideal path, but it would not be as empowering or satisfying. You alone have now improved the quality of this ideal frequency, along with the other four by this cleansing.

In addition, if you are not aware of this ideal path, your consciousness will remain on your current, less desirable frequency, and you will be denied this ideal option consciously. Your empowerment is your ability to switch tracks to this ideal frequency.

Quantum physicist Fred Alan Wolf states that there is something other than space-time, something not measurable and a redefinition of the laws of physics. It is pure consciousness. It is our alpha brain wave level (electromagnetic radiation), which is what we deal with in hypnotherapy. Conventional therapy refers to this alpha level as the subconscious. Wolf also states that the new physics tells us that our futures (and pasts) are influenced directly with thought. He states that this is not will, but awareness; what we visualize is what we see. There is no physical world without our thoughts about it. If we are "hung up" on the past, we may choose to see the future as we saw the past, and our self-defeating sequences (SDSs) may repeat themselves. If we alter our perception of the present via hypnotic programming, then our altered view may change the future. In other words, we can switch from a less attractive future path (frequency) to a more desirable one.[3]

Cleansing techniques along with positive hypnotic programming in the current awareness, supplemented by the patient's perception of and cleansing away of energy blocks (factors that lower the frequency vibration rate of our alpha brain wave level) incurred in the past can help place patients on a far more positive and productive path and their frequencies are raised.

Many dreams seem to contain fragments of futuristic material, just as they contain fragments from the past. In sleep, the mind appears to wander freely back and forth over the "equator," an imaginary line between the present and the future. At the deepest level of consciousness there is no sense of the flow of time, only an eternal now in which all events coexist. The future is capable of taking many possible final forms. Only when it congeals into the present does it really exist as an actuality.

An interesting sidelight of the idea that we dream the future as well as the past is that it offers an explanation for what is the most common of all psychic experiences: deja

---

[3] F. A. Wolf, *Taking the Quantum Leap* (New York: Harper & Row, 1981).

vu, "already seen." This is the strange sensation one sometimes has when encountering a new scene or situation that nevertheless seems oddly familiar. Deja vu may stem from precognitive dreams. If events that were fore-dreamed actually take place, we have the vague feeling that it has all happened to us before. However, we do not remember that we dreamed it. Studies have revealed that almost everyone dreams approximately three hours every night, but only a few of the dreams are remembered on awakening.

Returning to the concept of parallel universes or frequencies, Wolf points out that there are parallel universes in which exist human beings who may be exact duplicates of ourselves, and they may be connected to us through mechanisms available only through quantum physics. In these universes, different choices are being made at the same time you and I make our choices. The outcomes are different and thus the worlds are similar but still different. An indefinite number of futures and pasts can communicate with our present.

Hugh Everett was a graduate student in quantum physics at Princeton University who, in 1957, discovered the concept of parallel universes and used this concept as the basis of his dissertation for his doctorate. Wolf and others state that Everett's work showed that there are an infinite number of parallel universes. Wolf and Toben use Everett's metaphor of a flipped coin to illustrate the concept of parallel universes:

For example, when you flip a coin in the air, it lands with heads or tails showing, never both sides at the same time. But the coin's quantum wave always gives equal probability of heads or tails showing. How can the wave represent reality? Everett and his followers came up with the answer that for each possibility there exists a parallel universe where the event actually occurs. Thus, in one universe the coin lands heads and in another it lands tails. And even more surprising, you are in both universes observing the coin's fate! You exist in each world. Yet each world is essentially unknown to the other.[4]

Even though there are, theoretically, an infinite number of parallel universes (frequencies), my experience since 1977 with over five thousand progressions suggests that for human beings there are five main frequencies. That is, an infinite number of subfrequencies exist, but they seem to fall into five main categories and groups. Thus, you may have a million variations of frequency number 1, but the basic framework is similar. Frequencies number 2 through 5 will have very different frameworks or basic events but within each of these groups (frequencies) the framework is similar. Your five frequencies may be quite different from mine, depending upon your subconscious mind's (soul's) frequency vibrational rate (level of spiritual growth). Through progression hypnotherapy you can lay out these five paths, select the best one and be programmed for your most attractive future.

---

[4] F. A. Wolf and B. Toben, *Space-Time and Beyond* (New York: Bantam Books, 1982), p. 130.

The "New-You" Technique

I refer to the patients who have custom designed their own destiny by undergoing age progression, perceiving their five frequencies and selecting their ideal frequency as the "New-You" technique.

By having the patients perceive their future options in this life, they are empowered to be in control of their own destiny by selecting and being programmed to their ideal frequencies. I personally find this most rewarding. The fact that each and every one of my patients can control his or her own destiny is indeed fulfilling. It also most definitely fits within the theme of this book.

Since the patients have undergone cleansing prior to age progression, they have literally created their own reality and custom designed their future. Because your future circumstances are under your total control, *any* particular path is a possibility.

The quality of your current future frequency constantly changes based upon your present soul's energy level. I previously explained that once your soul or subconscious reaches a certain energy level, it cannot be lowered. It can either plateau at its current level or raise to a higher one.

You are in complete control of creating this ideal frequency. There are no limits to your potential. You may wish to be rich, famous, and successful at all you attempt; or you may be quite satisfied with a mere modest goal. The choice is yours. No right or wrong, no better or worse are involved in this exercise. The only referee is your Higher Self.

Because of your present focus, which concentrates so exclusively on information gained by conscious reasoning about the data supplied by the five senses, you may be reluctant to believe that one of the innate abilities of a human being is a type of time-travel within that individual's consciousness. This talent is innate and available to all of us.

Scientific breakthroughs use this mechanism. This flash of inspiration is not a cognitive process. The source of this intuition permeates our consciousness from our Higher Self. This intuitive break-through is something akin to compressing all that conscious reasoning time into a "time warp" that then bursts upon the scientist's consciousness in a flash of inspiration. As Thomas Edison so aptly put it, "Genius is one percent inspiration and 99 percent perspiration."

When you access your Higher Self and receive information concerning one of your future frequencies, knowledge not previously possessed by you will enter your awareness. Do not be alarmed by this. You may not even realize that these first few tidbits are indeed a result of contact with your future. It is natural to classify the results of every exercise as your imaginings. Eventually, however, you spot some things that, on reflection, look like new ideas that have a different "feel" to them. At that point you will say to yourself, "Well, I couldn't have made that up because I didn't consciously know the information beforehand."

It is with a little experience and validation that these future events you observed several months ago are now occurring, that confidence in this "New-You" technique finally emerges. Do not contaminate this method with preconceptions of what those attributes of the communication will actually be like. By doing so, you may hinder your recognition of the contact.

The communications from the future may be in the form of a dialogue you hear in your head, just as you hear physically spoken words with your ears. It may be that for you, the contact takes the form of "just knowing" some information came, and recognizing what the information was. It does not have to be in the form of some scene or visualization.

Another word of caution, about the "New-You" technique, concerns the big picture of the universe. Always maintain a high code of ethics when practicing your exercises and initiating subsequent actions. There are actions on your part that are contingent upon the actions of others. Your beliefs will draw those other souls necessary for you to successfully play your particular part and vice versa.

You undoubtedly will suffer some setbacks along the path to success, as I previously discussed. Your beliefs will create those circumstances that will challenge you in ways to your best advantage. You may encounter a particular difficulty on the road to your desired goal, but the lessons learned and advancements made from overcoming this difficulty will be requisite for your success.

Here is a script for age progression. I always recommend making tapes of these techniques. As I stated before, if you would like professionally recorded tapes feel free to contact my office for a comprehensive list of these titles.

Age Progression

Now listen very carefully. I want you to imagine a bright white light, coming down from above and entering the top of your head, filling your entire body. See it, feel it and it becomes reality. Now imagine an aura of pure white light emanating from your heart region, again surrounding your entire body, protecting you. See it, feel it and it becomes a reality. Now only your Higher Self, masters and guides, and highly evolved loving entities who mean you well will be able to influence you during this or any other hypnotic session. You are totally protected by this aura of pure white light. Focus carefully on my voice as your subconscious mind has memories of all past, present and future events. This tape will help guide you into the future. Shortly I am going to be counting forward from 1 to 20. Near the end of this count you are going to imagine yourself moving through a tunnel. Near the end of this count you will perceive the tunnel veering off to the left and to the right. The right represents the past; the left represents the future. On the count of 20 you will perceive yourself in the future. Your subconscious and superconscious mind levels have all the knowledge and information that you desire. Carefully and comfortably feel yourself moving into the future with each count from 1 to 20. Listen carefully now. If you have used this technique before and received information about one or more of your other frequencies, I want you to select a different one to explore. If you have already reviewed your five frequencies and would like to be programmed for your ideal frequency, simply concentrate on the number you have assigned to that ideal frequency and explore that particular path at this time.

Number 1, feel yourself now moving forward to the future, into this very, very deep and dark tunnel. 2, 3 - farther and farther and farther into the future. It is a little bit disorienting but you know you're moving into the future. 4, 5, 6, 7, 8, 9 - it's more stable now and you feel comfortable, you feel almost as if you're floating, as you're rising up and into the future. 10, 11, 12 - the tunnel is now getting a little bit lighter and you can perceive a light at the end, another white light just like the white light that is surrounding you. 13, 14, 15 - now you are almost there. Focus carefully. You can perceive in front of you a door to this left tunnel that you are in right now. The door will be opened in just a few moments and you will see yourself in the future. The words "sleep now and rest" will always detach you from any scene you are experiencing and allow you to await further instructions. 16, 17 - it's very bright now and you are putting your hands on the door. 18 - you open the door. 19 - you step into this future, to this future scene. 20 - carefully focus on your surroundings, look around you, see what you perceive. Can you perceive yourself? Can you perceive other people around you? Focus on the environment. What does it look like? Carefully focus on this. Use your complete objectivity. Block out any information from the past that might have interfered with the quality of the scene. Use only what your subconscious and superconscious mind level will observe. Now take a few moments, focus carefully on the scene, find out where you are and what you are doing, why are you there. Take a few moments; let the scene manifest itself.

Play New Age Music For 3 Minutes

Now focus very carefully on what year this is. Think for a moment. Numbers will appear before your inner eyes. You will have knowledge of the year that you are in right now. Carefully focus on this year and these numbers. They will appear before you. Use this as an example of other information that you are going to obtain. I want you to perceive this scene completely, carry it through to completion. I want you to perceive exactly where you are, who you are, the name, the date, the place. I want you to carry these scenes to completion, follow them through carefully for the next few moments. The scene will become clear and you will perceive the sequence of what exactly is happening to you.

Play New Age Music For 3 Minutes

You've done very well. Now you are going to move to another event. I want you to focus on a difference in the same future time and in the same frequency. Perceive what is going on and why this is important to you. Perceive the year, the environment, the presence of others. Let the information flow.

Play New Age Music For 3 Minutes

As you perceive the details of the next scene, also focus in on your purpose. Focus in on what you are learning, what you are unable to learn. Perceive any sequence of events that led up to this situation. Let the information flow surrounding this all-important future event now.

Play New Age Music For 3 Minutes

You have done very well. Now I want you to rise to the superconscious mind level to evaluate this future experience and apply this knowledge to other future frequencies and your current life and situations. 1 - rising up. 2 - rising higher.   3 - halfway there. 4 - almost there, 5 - you are there. Again, if you have decided that this is your ideal future path and want to be programmed to it, just concentrate on the number you have assigned to it and any significant events that separate it from the other frequencies.

If you are unsure of which is your ideal path, let your Higher Self assist you in making this choice and follow the instructions I previously gave.

Let your Higher Self assist you in making the most out of this experience. Do this now.

All right now. Sleep and rest. You did very well. Listen very carefully. I'm going to count forward now from 1 to 5. When I reach the count of 5 you will be back in the present, you will be able to remember everything you experienced and re-experienced. You'll feel very relaxed, refreshed, and you'll be able to do whatever you have planned for the rest of the day or evening. You'll feel positive about what you have just experienced and very motivated about your confidence and ability to play this tape again to experience additional future events. All right now. 1 - very, very deep. 2 - you're getting a little lighter. 3 - you're much, much lighter. 4 - very, very light. 5 - awaken.

The Case Of Marla

To illustrate the concept of frequencies and of selecting an ideal path, let us review my former patient Marla. Marla came to my Los Angeles office in the early part of 1990. This thirty-two-year-old secretary was depressed and saw no hope for her future. She was single and had a poor history of relationships with men. Marla wanted to raise a family.

The first step was to conduct "cleansing" sessions with Marla. This resulted in her raising the quality of her subconscious. This subconscious is, after all, electromagnetic radiation and can be purified.

After these cleansings were completed, Marla was ready for her progressions. The main purpose of the superconscious mind taps, or cleansing, is to raise the patients' subconscious mind level, which in turn increases the quality of each of their future frequencies. It also serves to empower them and improve their present status.

Marla's five frequencies can be summarized as follows:

Time Frame	Frequency	Event
1990-1995	1	Lose job and remain unemployed for 6 months. No functional relationship. Eventual new job pays less and is more stressful. Depression. Weight gain of 20 pounds.
	2	Same job. No significant change in patterns exhibited in current frequency. Occasional dating, but not serious relationship. Finances improve somewhat.
	3	Same job. Health problems emerge (skin disorder, insomnia). Long-term

relationship with a
man ends by 1994 in
frustration. Weight
gain of ten pounds.
Moves back to
Northern CA.

4

Meets a successful
businessman. One
year engagement.
Marries him and has
two children (son and
daughter). moves to
Brentwood. Very
happy. Loses eight
pounds. Opens up a
small boutique that
is very successful.

5

In 1992 meets an
actor. Good
relationship. They get
married and he quits
acting and is
employed with a
computer company.
She has one child.
Moderately happy,
but still has to work
in a job she doesn't
like.

It was not difficult for Marla to select her ideal frequency, which was number 4. Only one session was required to "switch tracks" and program her for this future path. Marla's spectrum was quite typical. Usually one of the frequencies is similar to her life now, and is her current path (number 2 in this example). One frequency is very poor (number 1) and another is below average (number 3). Still another frequency is very good (number 5), while only one is ideal (number 4).

As a follow-up, I called Marla to see how she was doing in the spring of 1996. Marla was married to Ted, a successful businessman, and she was the proud mother of a 3 1/2-year-old son and 2-year-old daughter. They lived in Brentwood and Marla owns a small boutique that is doing quite well. As Shakespeare said, "All's well that ends well."

Einstein demonstrated that matter and energy are really the same thing with his famous equation $E = MC^2$. At certain speeds, physical objects cease to be physical objects as we know them, but fields of electrical force or energy. If an object could travel with the speed of light it would be transformed into light!

If, as with precognition, we are bemused by time, it is not surprising and nothing to feel depressed about. We happen to be upon the Earth, but in other parts of the universe time means something different. Something happening in what we call "the present" could be seen in different parts of the universe at totally different times, according to the distance of the vantage points of the different observers. The time taken for light to travel to different parts of the universe could differ by billions of years. By the same token, time becomes nonsense when we look through a telescope. To us the time is now. Now we can see Andromeda, two million light years away. What happened two million years ago and what happened three hundred years ago appear to us at the same moment. For what we see has traveled toward us with the speed of light, and has taken those differing periods to do so.

The further you look out into space, the farther you travel back in time. Time means no more than an opportunity for things to change and for persons to strive - the possibility of progress and improvement. "Reality" is experienced, not as something lasting or everlasting, but timeless. The consequences of your life depend on you alone. You are always in control of your own destiny.

Chapter 13
Assertive Training

Assertiveness is a necessary step in your goal to custom design your own destiny. A good definition of assertiveness is a series of skills that allow you to communicate your position and negative feelings honestly and directly with others. Anyone can master these skills with practice.

Basically, assertiveness entails being aware of your rights as a human being and speaking and acting in a manner to protect those rights. You will suddenly find yourself being able to say no without guilt, to ask for what you want directly, and in general to communicate more clearly and openly in all your relationships. Your self-confidence will improve dramatically, and you will develop an awareness and respect for the rights of others. Always remember that people don't care how much you know until they know how much you care.

Before I discuss assertive behavior in detail, it is important for you to understand two other (and dysfunctional) behavior styles. These are passive behavior and aggressive behavior.

Passive Behavior

A person is behaving passively when he lets others push him around, when he does not stand up for himself, and when he does what he is told regardless of how he feels about it. The advantage of being passive is that you rarely experience direct rejection. The disadvantage is that you are taken advantage of, and you store up a heavy burden of resentment and anger.

Examples of passive behavior are the use of expressions such as:

- "I don't matter - my feelings, rights, opinions and ideas aren't important."
- "I mean" and "You know."
- "I don't know if anyone will agree with this."
- "This is only my opinion."

Aggressive Behavior

Typical examples of aggressive behavior are fighting, accusing, threatening and generally stepping on people without regard for their feelings. The advantage of this kind of behavior is that people do not push the aggressive person around. The disadvantage is that people do not want to be around him or her. Sometimes aggressive people point fingers accusingly, or make broad gestures with their hands that intrude on other people's space. Like children, aggressive people are usually ignorant of or unconcerned about the damage they are causing to their relationships.

Assertive Behavior

Jack Nicholson illustrated one of the classic examples of assertive behavior in the feature film *Five Easy Pieces*. In a restaurant Jack cannot convince the waitress to bring him just a side order of toast. It's not on the menu. His imaginative solution is to order a chicken salad sandwich with the following instructions: no mayonnaise, keep the butter on it and hold the chicken.

A person is behaving assertively when he stands up for himself, expresses his true feelings, and does not let others take advantage of him. At the same time, he is considerate of others' feelings. The advantage of being assertive is that you get what you want, usually without making others angry.

If you are assertive, you can act in your own best interest and not feel guilty or wrong about it. Meekness and withdrawal, attack and blame are no longer needed with the mastery of assertive behavior. They are seen for what they are - sadly inadequate strategies of escape that create more pain and stress than they prevent. Before you can achieve assertive behavior, you must really face the fact that the passive and aggressive styles have often failed to get you what you want.

Assertive Bill Of Rights

1. It is your right to do anything as long as you do not purposely hurt someone else and you are willing to accept the consequences.
2. It is your right to maintain your self-respect by answering honestly even if it does hurt someone else. This only applies to your being assertive, not aggressive.
3. It is your right to be what you are without changing your ideas or behavior to satisfy someone else.
4. It is your right to strive for self-fulfillment.
5. It is your right to use your own judgment as to the need priorities of yourself and others, if you decide to accept any responsibility for another's problems.
6. It is your right not to be subjected to negativity. It is your right to offer no excuses or justifications for your decisions or behavior.
7. It is your right not to care.
8. It is your right to be illogical.
9. It is your right to change your mind.
10. It is your right to defend yourself without feeling self-conscious.
11. You have a right to negotiate for change.
12. You have a right to ask for help or emotional support.
13. You have a right to feel and express pain.

14. You have a right to ignore the advice of others.
15. You have a right to receive formal recognition for your work and achievements.
16. You have a right to say "no."
17. You have a right to be alone, even if others would prefer your company.
18. You have a right not to have to justify yourself to others.
19. You have a right not to take responsibility for someone else's problem.
20. You have the right to assert yourself even though you may inconvenience others.
21. You have the right to be listened to and taken seriously.
22. You have the right to set your own priorities.
23. You have the right to ask for what you want.
24. You have the right to get what you pay for.
25. You have a right not to anticipate others' needs and wishes.
26. You have a right not to always worry about the goodwill of others.
27. You have a right to choose not to respond to a situation.
28. You have a right to sometimes put yourself first.
29. You have a right to make mistakes.
30. You have a right to be the final judge of your feelings and accept them as legitimate.
31. You have a right to have your own opinions and convictions.

32. You have a right to protest unfair treatment or undue criticism.
33. You have a right to interrupt in order to ask for clarification.

The first step in adopting an assertive behavior style is behavioral change. There are six steps in making a functional change in behavior. These are:

1. Identify problems in your current behavior. What outcomes is that behavior creating?
2. Set goals for your new behavior. What new results would you like to achieve? Visualizing the change can give you the motivation to try new behaviors.
3. Identify the beliefs, attitudes, and feelings that are
   keeping your existing behavior in place.
4. Acquire new skills. You will need practical skills that will reinforce your new behavior and keep you from reverting to old patterns.
5. Practice. This is the most important step. Gradually phase in these empowering behavioral patterns.
6. Note your positive experiences. Reward yourself after you have had a success.

We discussed the self-image in chapter 7. The following exercise will assist you in building up your self-image and strengthening your goal to become assertive:

1. Record your successes every day. Keep a journal and review it often.
2. Acknowledge other people. Building up the self-esteem of others will benefit both you and them.
3. Smile at yourself as often as you can. Use a portable mirror to visually obtain feedback on this simple yet effective technique.
4. Dress and look your best. This can go a long way toward helping you build up your self-image.

Becoming assertive also means changing your old, inappropriate beliefs. This occurs in four steps:

1. Identifying a situation in which you are not as assertive as you would like to be.
2. Identifying the belief underlying your nonassertive behavior.
3. Visualizing yourself behaving more confidently and assertively in that situation.
4. Making up (creating) one or more new beliefs that you would have to accept in order to practice the desired assertive behavior.

Avoiding Being Manipulated

Another step to becoming an assertive person is learning how to avoid manipulation. Inevitably, you are will encounter blocking gambits from those who seek to ignore your assertive requests. The following techniques are proven ways of overcoming the standard blocking gambits.

1.   **Broken Record or Repeat Techniques**. Ignore the attempts to manipulate, and repeat what you want in a calm voice. Continue repeating what you want until the other person consents or you arrive at a compromise.

2.   **"I"-First Statements.** Know what you want and respond to your "I" needs by saying "I. . . ." . These statements should be straightforward and clear. You will find that by using these statements there is less likelihood that other people will continue to try to manipulate you. Do not apologize or demean yourself when formulating "I" statements.

3.   **Assertive Agreement.** In admitting a mistake or a fault, simply agree with the other person's criticism without apologizing for it. Do not take the blame for something that is someone else's responsibility, or if you truly believe that you are correct.

4.   **Clouding.** If you see someone attempting to sidetrack or cloud an issue, be firm and demand a direct answer. Use the repeat technique with "I" statements. Appear to give ground without actually doing so. Agree with the person's argument, but don't agree to change. ("You may be right, I probably could be more generous. Perhaps I shouldn't be so confrontational, but. . .")

5.   **Defusing.** Ignoring the content of someone's anger, and putting off further discussion until he has calmed down. "I can see that you're very upset and angry right now, let's discuss it later this afternoon."

6. **Circuit Breaker.** Responding to provocative criticism with one word, or very clipped statements. ("Yes. . . no. . .perhaps.")

7. **Assertive Irony.** Responding to hostile criticism positively. (Respond to, "You're a real loudmouth" with "Thank you.")

8. **Assertive Delay.** Putting off a response to a challenging statement until you are calm and able to deal with it appropriately. ("Yes. . .very interesting point . . .I'll have to reserve judgment on that. . .I don't want to talk about that right now.")

9. **Assertive Inquiry.** Prompting criticism in order to gather additional information for your side of the argument. ("I understand you don't like the way I acted at the meeting last night. What is it about it that bothers you?")

10. **Content-to-Process Shift.** Shifting the focus of the discussion from the topic to an analysis of what is going on between the two of you. ("We're getting off the point now. You appear to be angry with me.")

It is helpful to prepare yourself against a number of typical blocking gambits that will be used to attack and derail your assertive requests. Some of the most troublesome blocking gambits include:

1. **Laughing It Off.** Your assertion is responded to with a joke. ("Only three weeks late? I've got to work on being less punctual!") Use the Content-to-Process

Shift ("Humor is getting us off the point.") and the Broken Record (Yes, but. . .").

2. **Accusing Gambit.** You are blamed for the problem. ("You are always so late cooking dinner, I'm too tired to do the dishes afterward.") Use Clouding ("That may be so, but you are still breaking your commitment.") or simply disagree ("8:00 is not too late for the dishes.").

3. **The Beat-Up.** Your assertion is responded to with a personal attack, such as "Who are you to worry about being interrupted, you are the biggest loudmouth around here." The best strategies to use are Assertive Irony ("Thank you") in conjunction with the Broken Record or Defusing ("I can see you're angry right now, let's talk about it after the meeting.").

4. **Delaying Gambit.** Your assertion is met with, "Not now, I'm too tired" or "Another time, maybe." Use the Broken Record or insist on setting a specific time when the problem can be discussed.

5. **Why Gambit.** Every assertive statement is blocked with a series of "why" questions, such as, "Why do you feel that way. . .I still don't know why you don't want to go. . .Why did you change your mind?" The best response is to use the Content-to-Process Shift ("Why isn't the point. The issue is that I'm not willing to go tonight.") or the Broken Record.

6. **Self-Pity Gambit.** Your assertion is met with tears and the covert message that you are being sadistic. Try to keep going through your script using

Assertive Agreement. ("I know this is causing you pain, but I need to get this resolved.")

7. **Quibbling.** The other person wants to debate with you about the legitimacy of what you feel, or the magnitude of the problem, etc. Use the Content-to-Process Shift. ("We're quibbling now, and have gotten off the main concern.") with the assertion of you're right to feel the way you do.

8. **Threats.** You are threatened with statements like, "If you keep harping at me like this, you're going to need another boy-friend." Use the Circuit Breaker ("Perhaps") and Assertive Inquiry ("What is it about my requests that bother you?") as well as Content-to-Process Shift ("This seems to be a threat.") or Defusing.

9. **Denial.** You are told, "I didn't do that" or "You've really misinterpreted me." Assert what you have observed and experienced and use Clouding. ("It may seem that way to you, but I've observed. . .")

Saying "No"

One of the best techniques in handling an attempt by someone to victimize you is simply to say "NO." You could always rely on the "What is it about no you don't understand?" You can tell the other person that you appreciate how important the activity is to him but you are too busy to help him out now. It is critical that you don't apologize for your decision.

Many people find it difficult to say no. They spend too much time on other people's priorities and are fearful of standing up for their own. By saying "yes" often there is little hope of doing what is asked of you. A "yes" may actually mean "maybe," and this will undoubtedly eventually wind up becoming a "no," or in your being unable to complete the task you were pressured to comply with. To do this is simply poor ethics, poor business, poor personal relations, and it can make life harder for everyone in the future.

Here are some steps in preparing to say no to a request that you were pressured to agree to:

1. Choose the relationship or situation you want to work on.

2. Think about your reasons for saying yes. Are you trying to please? Do you think saying no will injure the relationship? Do you think you will hurt the other person's feelings?

3. Decide what you want in the situation. Get very clear about your preferences.

4. Think about what the other person wants, and what he or she may accept from you as a counteroffer or substitute for the request.

5. Practice the conversation in advance. Practice is the key to all forms of assertive training.

Body Language

Body language is a form of nonverbal communication. The information I presented in the beginning of this chapter depicting the passive, aggressive and assertive behavior styles gave you an introduction to this concept. We will now discuss this principle in greater detail.

In general an individual is exerting self-control when he sits with hands clasped and resting on his stomach. Leaning back in a chair with both hands behind the head indicates a contemplative or relaxed assertive posture. If this individual ran her index finger up along the side of her nose or up to the nose with the remaining fingers curled under and the thumb positioned under the chin, a critical evaluation is being suggested. Another gesture that indicates thinking about an idea is when someone strokes his chin.

If you communicate with someone who is touching his fingertips and pulling his palms apart to form a church steeple, this individual is confident of what he is saying. A person sitting with her arms crossed on her chest is expressing her fixed and unmovable stance on whatever you are discussing. If he or she also sits with legs crossed, well back in the chair, you have a real adversary on your hands.

Body Language Suggesting Anxiety

When individuals are nervous, frustrated, suspicious, or just ill at ease, they will exhibit the following body positions:

- Arms crossed on the chest indicating a defensive and closed state of mind.

- The palm of their hand placed on the back of their neck, suggesting guilt.
- Rubbing or touching the nose while talking indicating the speaker is lying or very unsure about what he or she is saying.
- A woman placing her hand to her throat indicates she needs reassurance.
- Wringing of the hands indicates extreme anxiety.
- Covering the mouth with the hands while speaking indicates self-doubt or a lie.
- Hands clenched tightly suggest defiance and suspicion.
- Turning the body away from you at approximately a 45-degree angle means a clear "no."
- Slumped shoulders indicate depression.
- Ankles locked when the person is seated indicate repression of feelings.
- Positioning the body to face the door suggests this individual wants to leave as soon as possible.
- Tugging at one's ear while listening to another person speak represents a desire to interrupt.
- Other body mannerisms indicating anxiety are repetitive gestures, a rigid stance, clearing the throat and fidgeting in the chair.

It is important to understand these so you can properly assess other people's body language and recognize these characteristics in yourself.

The following body positions and mannerisms are indicative of positive and assertive behavior.

- A firm handshake.
- Sitting on the edge of a chair indicates cooperation and a willingness to initiate action.
- Open hands indicate openness and sincerity.
- Thumb tucked under the belt suggests everything is under control.
- Unbuttoning the coat indicates a receptive attitude.
- A slightly tilted head suggests this person is interested in what you are saying.
- Touching gestures indicate warmth.
- A deliberate and positive walk with the shoulders back, chin up and body fully erect shows confidence and strength.
- Slight nodding of the head indicates this person is in agreement with you.
- Leaning forward in the chair suggests a real interest in what is being presented.

It is important to consider several gestures and body positions before you come to a conclusion about what type of individual you are dealing with. Practice will make you more aware, accurate and confident about reading people through their nonverbal communication. There are several books listed in the bibliography that will give you a more comprehensive treatment of this fascinating aspect of our psyche.

Taking assertive action is not difficult once you log in a few successful experiences. Here is a checklist to assist you in assertive action behavior:

Take the initiative. Pick a time and setting when you feel in control. Avoid discussions when you feel uncomfortable or distracted.

Make sure your nonverbal communication (body language) reinforces your verbal statements. Maintain good eye contact. Speak audibly and firmly.

Tune in to the way your body feels. Let physical discomforts in your body be an indicator that something is wrong.

Get to the point simply and directly without a lot of distracting preliminaries. Never assume the other person will automatically understand your meaning.

Describe your feelings without attacking the other person's behavior. Use "I" statements rather than "you" statements for example, "I am not happy with your handling the assignment late," rather than "You never complete assignments on time!"

Don't ask questions unless you want the answer.

Decide what you want to say and how you want to say it. Rehearse difficult conversations and have notes if it is to be communicated by phone.

If you are responding to a request:

- Answer promptly and to the point.

- Don't over-explain. Learn when to stop talking.
- Never apologize for your decision.
- If a request seems unreasonable, say so, and try to focus on the area of conflict. Don't propose a compromise unless you're willing to make certain concessions.

Communication Principles

The following principles will help you be a more effective communicator.

- For easy communication action, there will be some receiver reaction.
- Making a hasty remark or giving someone a quick putdown may have little effect in the short run, but it will certainly affect your long-term relationship and future interactions.
- One person's thoughts are attracted to another person's thoughts with a force directly proportionate to the similarity of their experience. We are attracted to people who we think are like us. The problem is that people are a mixture of hundreds of different experiences, and often we make the mistake of thinking they're just like us. In many subtle and larger ways they aren't.
- In order to have others see things your way, you must first see things their way. Every good negotiator and salesperson knows this. You

must tune in to their needs, motivations, concerns, and preferences before you can get them to adopt your position.

- You must have the other person's attention and interest before reasoning and communication can begin. You should be flexible enough to attend to their specific needs; know whatever attention-getter works best for each specific individual.

Win/Win/Win Communication

To be truly assertive, all your communication should have as its goal win (you), win (the other person) and win (the universe) mentality. This way everyone gets what he or she wants and there are no losers.

There are three key elements in win/win/win thinking:

1.   Aiming at a result or goal that will enable both you and the other person to get what you want.

2.   Caring that the other person gets the results he or she wants.

3.   Being open to changing your goal, if necessary, to avoid a win/win/lose trap.

Managing stress is an important part of being assertive. If you can relax and keep life's daily stresses to a minimum, you will do wonders to your self-image and have more energy and motivation to accomplish your goals. Here are some tips to help you reduce stress:

- When you know you have to refuse someone, say no right away. Apply this to tasks and invitations.
- Allow extra time for everything. Arrive early.
- Write angry letters and rip them up.
- Don't rely on memory for addresses or telephone numbers of your appointments.
- Always carry "waiting work" or a good book to read so lines or travel do not frustrate you.
- Double-check meeting places, times and dates.
- Look for some humorous aspect to any uncomfortable situation.
- Keep extra supplies of pens, stamps, pads and other frequently used items.

Setting Limits

Assertive people always have limits. This is their "line in the sand," beyond which they don't compromise. The higher your   self-image, the more disciplined you are at keeping these limits. Setting limits tells people who you are and instructs them how you want to be treated.

The following simple rules will assist you in establishing your own limits:

- Delineate your limits precisely. Let the other person know exactly and specifically what your limits are in a particular situation.
- Set partial limits. Those parameters need not be an all-or-nothing proposition.

- Be firm. This is critical because if you permit this limit to be violated, you will lose self-respect and credibility in the other person's eyes.
- Detach yourself from the reactions of others to your limits. You are not responsible for other people's feelings.

Remember, nobody has the right to take advantage of or manipulate another human being. You, and only you, are responsible for positive changes in your life and increasing your assertiveness. Once you change even one behavioral pattern you change a whole series of related behaviors. It can and will be the beginning of a whole new lifestyle and the beginning of your custom designing your own destiny.

Chapter 14
Consciousness Expansion

We are most definitely more than just a physical body. When we access our Higher Self and practice the "New-You" technique, we are removing ourselves from space-time constraints. Whether you are using hypnosis, meditation or other relaxation methods to get in touch with your nonphysical energy, you are now using mind to create your reality. Properly trained, anyone can custom design one's own destiny.

Some refer to this nonphysical energy as prana, Chi, Astral body, higher consciousness and so on. Whatever you call it (I prefer the superconscious mind), consciousness is a form of energy that allows you to transform yourself and your world by changing old beliefs, raising the quality of your soul's energy and introducing you to the limitless potential of your Higher Self.

These techniques allow you to answer such questions as, "What is my purpose?" and "How can I become empowered?" Because alpha states produce expanded states of consciousness, the resulting transcendent states cannot easily be described. You are now traveling beyond the subconscious into a universal awareness that can literally transform your reality at your direction.

The future aspect (age progression) of the "New-You" technique should not be treated lightly. There are endless illustrations of what seems to be the uncanny precognition of some people; they have intuition.

Beginning in 1962, at the PSI Communications Project of the Newark College of Engineering, research has continued involving ESP and success in business.[1] The project has tested over 9,000 business executives to determine whether there is any correlation between a person's ability to make successful decisions in a business context and his ability to intuit data on a series of cards. The results have been surprising; a primary conclusion from the PSI Project data is that the most successful executives must call on other sources of "information" than what is apparently obvious to them at the moments of their decision-making.

The work of C. Honorton verifies the conclusions of the PSI Project and erases any doubts we might have about the brain wave states most conducive to ESP sensitivities. Steady low-frequency alpha brain waves, and occasionally

---

[1] J. Mihalasky and D. Dean, "PSI Research." (Newark: Newark College of Engineering, 1971).

theta waves, appear on the EEGs of most successful telepathic subjects when they are engaged in experiments[2]

All intelligent beings, humans and some of the higher animals, live in three worlds of time: the past, the present and the future. The present is, of course, obvious. But some think we live only in the present. A moment's reflection will prove to you that this is not so. True, we act only in the present, but in memory we live in the past. In fact, the past exerts a major influence on our present existence because our acts and the events that have occurred to us in the past have created our present. Our thoughts today and our inclination toward this or that line of conduct are the product of all our experiences up to the moment of action.

We likewise live in the future, but to a lesser degree. And this, too, has an influence on our actions today though not as great an influence as the habit patterns set up in the past. We read the weather report and decide we should take a coat when leaving the house. We buy a cake because we expect visitors for dinner. We save money for the future. We buy insurance. The future influences us in hundreds of ways.

To some degree, at least, an estimate of the future influences all our plans and actions. We do not decide ourselves. We know we are not dealing with certainties, only with probabilities. But these vary from highly probable to scarcely possible, and we permit them to influence our

---

[2] C. Honorton, "Relationship between EEG alpha activity and ESP card guessing performance" *Journal of the American Society for Psychical Research* 63 (1969): 365-374.

actions according to our estimate of their probability. We base these estimates on the information we possess, and the more information at hand, the more accurate our prognosis will be. Sometimes a very careful person will sit at a desk and write down all the pros and cons before making a judgment. But most of us rely entirely on the computer-like speed with which our minds balance these out and reach conclusions. The foregoing refers to predictions based upon knowledge obtained through one or more of the five physical senses and stored in the brain. But we frequently act upon knowledge we have acquired in some other fashion. In addition to intuition, which many people lean on quite heavily, extrasensory perception and telepathic rapport guide most of us to some extent whether we realize it or not.

Here is a simple ESP exercise to introduce you to consciousness expansion:

Close your eyes and endeavor to "see" the time on your watch or the clock nearest you without looking at it. The very instant the image of the clock face with the position of the hands appears before you, note the time and open your eyes.

Don't think about it. If you start to think, a reasoning process begins, which destroys the experiment. This reasoning is done in and by the physical brain and the purpose of the experiment is to take your awareness directly to the second level, bypassing the physical brain, and make observations there.

You may succeed in this quite quickly, or it may take you several days and many attempts before you can get a correct reading on demand. Most of us are so in the habit of "guessing" the time from our estimate of how much time may have elapsed since last we looked, or from observations of the light, or the sounds, or any number of other physical phenomena, that we automatically in this way start to reason with ourselves instead of going directly to the higher level for a "look." So it may take a little time and effort for you to free yourself enough to make a direct approach to reality.

Once you can "tell time" in this manner, you will be able to accept more readily the more advanced techniques for approach to higher levels of consciousness. It is easy to go into the thought world, to think. It is just as easy to raise your consciousness into the causal world and observe there the myriad causes that influence every action, every decision. Just as the person on top of the tall building is aware of more facts, more potential causes, than are the drivers of the automobiles approaching the intersection below and can therefore say with fair certainty there will be a collision, so will you be able to foretell the future possibilities inherent in those causes you observe.

To effectively expand your consciousness, there are four essential steps that must be mastered. These are:

1. **Confidence**. You must know that you can raise your consciousness to higher levels. This confidence is developed through repeated successful experiments.

2. **Focused Awareness**. Once a level above the physical is attained, your consciousness is exposed to vast numbers of impacts that are confusing until distinguished. The second essential, therefore, is the ability to focus your

attention on those causes (and only those causes) that may bear upon the subject concerning you at the moment.

3. **Discrimination.** Even after you have successfully disassociated the prime causes from all others, it then becomes necessary to turn the light of your interest upon the more significant, those of highest probable impact upon the future, and allow the others to fade into the background.

4. **Judgment.** Having selected the most relevant causes through discrimination, it is then required that you reach a conclusion or form a judgment based upon those causes. This is not a simple task because even after all the foregoing sifting and culling out the less important, there may still be several thousand influences to be considered.

The ancient Egyptians in their temple referred to it as learning how "to build the bridge." Let me explain to you what this means. Let's assume you are attending one of my workshops. Right now, as you sit before me, you are using your physical faculties, your ears and eyes, to record all impressions they bring to your active, waking mind. My words enter your ears and are led to your brain where they are then associated with other similar ideas before being registered in your memory. You can observe this process and will recognize it as comparable to what always takes place when a sound or smell or any other agitation of the world about you impinges on one or more of your five physical senses.

But you get information in other ways - through the use of your sixth sense, or ESP. The following exercise is a simple training to give you an introduction to your psychic abilities:

When retiring for the night, preferably just before you drop off to sleep, tell yourself what you want and ask yourself to provide the answer. To a person who has never done this and knows nothing about the possibilities inherent in a human being this may sound impossible or even ridiculous. Yet this is exactly what you are to do.

For example, if you have misplaced your favorite ballpoint pen, say to yourself in words, "I want to locate my pen. Show me where it is." This is a very simple command and the instruction to yourself will work nine times out of ten.

When you waken, whether in the morning or before the night is over, write down immediately what you recall of your dream. For this you should have a notebook and a pencil or pen at your bedside. Write down everything you remember no matter how strange or even trivial it may seem. If you don't remember what you dreamed, tell yourself before sleeping the next night to remember, then you will.

Sometimes your dream, as remembered, will be quite definite and you will have no trouble understanding its meaning. Much more often it will appear to have no connection with the request you have made and in those instances you must think about your dream until you get the necessary clue.

This is the reason why most precognitive visions (age progressions) seem like memories to the person who records them. It is also the reason why symbols are so often used. When the brain does not have adequate nerve cells for the impression the Higher Self wishes to make, symbolism is usually employed. These subtle impacts upon the brain often go unnoticed although the Higher Self and subconscious mind are always trying to guide and help us. But when you are asleep and your brain is in a receptive state, the defense mechanisms do not now function. When you awake it is important that you remember what you were taught or shown so get into the habit of writing down every dream as soon as possible after waking. If you do not you will forget it within an hour. And don't just limit yourself to trying to recall your dream when you have asked for advice. Every morning make a record of what you remember. This will serve two purposes, both good. It will enable you to recall more and more of what you dreamed because you will become more proficient with practice. And, what may be more important, crucial advice or a serious warning might sometimes surface even though it was not specifically requested.

It is possible to ask yourself questions concerning the future and obtain accurate predictions. It is well to remember, however, that the inner self is quite literal minded, so phrase your question properly. For example, it would be a mistake to ask, "Will my brother get the job he is seeking?" You are thinking of a job with an automotive company where you know he has applied. What you do not know is that he has also applied for a position in three other companies. But your inner self knows and is therefore handicapped in giving a good reply. Your question should be phrased, "Will my brother get the job with the Ford Motor Company for which he has applied?" This is a specific question to which a clear-cut answer can be given.

It is true that a highly developed person can get answers to very complex requests, but for you, a beginner, simplicity and accuracy will bring much more satisfactory results.

Here is a slightly advanced exercise to access the Higher Self and get a glimpse into your future:

1. Sit, preferably in a straight-back chair so that your spine is held straight and your head erect. Avoid slumping or leaning to one side. Close your eyes and imagine you are in a motion picture theater all alone. Before you is a giant screen, absolutely blank. See it so in your mind's eye.

2. The screen is illuminated by a great white light so now you are looking at a completely blank huge white screen. Within a fraction of a second other images will start to crowd in, some on the screen, some on the periphery of your vision. With these intruders will come sounds, memories and desire fantasies. These must be pushed back - all of them, the sights, sounds, smells, feelings, everything, so that only the blank white screen remains. This is not easy and will require concentration, willpower and lots of practice before you will be able to hold the image of the screen, clear and unsullied, before your mind's eye for as long as five seconds. Once you are able to exclude everything from your awareness but the brilliant lit white screen for a solid five seconds, you are then ready for the next step.

3. Now carry yourself right into the white brightness of the screen so that it is all around you. At this point you will probably experience a pleasurable tingling on the surface of your skin. For the present, this must be ignored if you are to achieve the results you are striving for. When you are quite sure this scintillating brightness is all around you and you are conscious of nothing else, no stray thoughts, no sensations, no emotional fantasies of any kind, you are then in attunement with your Higher Self and have developed yourself to a point where you can consciously seek out information available to it.

4. When you become familiar with this state and can attain it at will, you are then ready to suggest certain things to yourself or ask for information in the same way you previously asked it on retiring. The difference here is that after making the request you proceed as quickly as possible to the state of conscious attunement with your Higher Self where answers will come in picture form (usually) just as they did in your dreams.

These next exercises are even more advanced, and will result in higher levels of consciousness expansion. Precede this with a   self-hypnosis induction:

Visualize yourself dreaming late at night. You now get out of bed and walk across the room to a closet. There is a door in the back of this closet that opens up to bring a stone staircase into your line of sight.

It is a very ancient-looking stone staircase, winding down and around, and in the dim light you begin going down the staircase, not at all afraid, but eager to go down, deeper and deeper, descending on down through the dream, going always deeper as you go down a step at a time, until finally reaching the bottom of the stairway to stand at the edge of what you recognize to be dark water, lapping, where a small boat is tied.

And now, lying on blankets in the bottom of the boat, the boat adrift and floating in blackness, dark all around, but rocking gently from the motion of the water, back and forth and rising and falling, gently rocked as the boat drifts on and on, as the boat drifts down and down, as you feel only that gentle rocking, listening to the lapping of the water, nearing an opening where the boat moves along toward a light at the opening, and passes out of the opening and into a warm sunlight.

Still floating, downstream, feeling the warm sunlight, and a soft breeze that passes over you, as you drift down and down, and along the bank the birds are singing, and the fish are jumping in the water, and there is the smell of flowers and of the freshly cut grass in fields that have just been mowed. Feeling a great contentment, serenity, drifting drowsily down and down, down and down, with that gentle rocking, and now just let your self feel it for a while. Be aware of this whole situation, the movements, the warmth, the sounds, the odors, as you keep on drifting down, down and down.

Continuing now to float, to rock gently, drifting deeper and deeper, until your boat approaches the shore and runs smoothly aground at the edge of a meadow. Leaving the boat now, and walking through the meadow, the grass against your legs, the breezes on your body, and conscious of rabbits in the tall grass, of the smell of the flowers all around, of birds singing in the trees, of the movements of your body as you walk, approaching a large tree and seating yourself beneath it, in its shade.

But now, for a while, just feel your surroundings, be in total harmony with all that exists here in this world out of time, this world without separations, this world where all is one, where you are one with all that is.

Ideal Body Image

This exercise can be used to lose weight, eliminate skin problems, improve posture, look younger ("youthing": see chapter 15), remove depression and so on. First practice the basic self-hypnosis exercise, and use the following script:

Mentally see an image of yourself standing before you. This is your body exactly as you would like it to appear, exactly as you want that body to be, and as it has the possibility of being. Look at it more and more closely now, and it will be a realistic but ideal body image, one that you really could achieve, and one that you will achieve. And when you have a very clear image of your body as you would like to have it, keep observing that image, and make it a part of your own reality.

Play New Age Music For 4 Minutes.

That ideal body image is becoming more and more real, you are seeing it very clearly, and seeing it in its full size and dimensions, and now you are going to step forward and into that body, you will find yourself in that body, so that you can try it out and make certain that it is just the body you do want to have, and if there is something you would like to change, then make those changes now.

Move around in that body, feel its strength and agility, its dynamic aliveness, its surging vitality, and make really certain that its appearance and all of its attributes are what you realistically desire. And, as you occupy that body, coming to know that body very well, your present physical body is going to be drawn into that new mold. You are moving already toward the realization of that ideal body image, and you will be doing whatever is needed to achieve that body you want to have.

Play New Age Music For 5 Minutes.

Whenever you desire to reenter into this wonderfully relaxing state of self-hypnosis, all you have to do is say the number 20 three times in succession - 20, 20, 20 and feel yourself sinking down into a deep relaxation.

When you are totally relaxed, you will be able to recreate this ideal body image.

End this trance as usual.

This next consciousness expansion exercise is designed to increase artistic creativity. We all have hobbies, and they should not be neglected. You can use this script as a model for any hobby that you have been ignoring because you feel you are blocked, or just lack the requisite skills:

And you will go deeper and deeper into trance, deeper and deeper, aware only of the voice that speaks to you, and of your own experiences as you move inward, inside of your-self, moving into realms inside of yourself where your talents and capacities are accessible to you as symbolic forms and personifications.

Deeper and deeper, and into that place, looking for and finding that personification representing the talent that you have for artistic work, for drawing, or painting, or sculpting, that kind of artistic work. You will know and firmly believe that everyone has some capacity to be an artist, although in some people this capacity has been severely inhibited and may be deeply buried. All people are not equally talented, but you do have the capacity to be a much more imaginative and effective artist than you have been in the past, and you will now find that ability personified, you will find the artist within yourself.

And let that artist personality expand now, dominating and filling your whole consciousness, so that you are the artist, and you will be able, without distraction and with the fullest access to your talent, to carry out the tasks that will be assigned to you.

And now for the next minute see yourself meeting a most exceptional artist who is also a very good art teacher, and this teacher will ask you to draw. You, the artist, will draw, and then you will receive from this teacher instruction about how to make your artwork more effective. You will practice, doing more drawings, receiving more criticism and instruction, and benefiting from it, and you will have all of these experiences beginning now!

This visualization exercise will sharpen your ability to access your Higher Self, and protect you from psychic attacks:

(a) Breathe in to a measured count of ten. As you inhale, concentrate on the center between the eyes until you can almost feel it. At the same time visualize it glowing with a golden light. This should not be the dull sheen of metallic gold but more like the brilliance of golden sunshine.

(b) Next hold your breath in for the count of 20 and at the same time concentrate on the center in the middle of your head. Visualize it surrounded by an aura of brilliant white light.

(c) Now breathe out in the same cadence to the count of twelve. As you do, visualize the white light blending with the golden light to form a huge aura of golden white light about your head.

(d) Repeat this exercise three times at each daily sitting for 30 days and five times at each sitting thereafter.

Here are three final exercises for consciousness expansion:

1. Sit erect in a straight-backed chair in a place where you will not be disturbed. Using your right hand place the forefinger directly on the center of your forehead about one inch above the bridge of your nose. Then place your thumb on the right side of your nose near the right eye and your middle finger on the left side almost as if you were grasping the upper part of your nose between your thumb and third finger. Maintain this position as you take a deep breath and hold it for the count of ten. As you do, feel the energy running down your right arm, into your hand and down your index finger into your head. Then exhale and without moving your hand repeat the exercise five times. This is designed to stimulate the pituitary gland and encourage attunement between it and the pineal gland in the center of the head. These glands are the physical terminals of your two major head centers. When they are in resonance with each other, the centers will coalesce and bring you a higher sense of awareness. Practice this every day.

2. Sit in a straight-backed chair or lie flat on a bed, or on the ground in a place where you will not be disturbed. Visualize a cloud of white light - like

*brilliant sunlight - above your head. This cloud should
be an oval about six feet high from top to bottom. Spend
as much time as you need in getting this clearly etched
in your consciousness. After all invading thoughts and
images have been shielded out take a deep breath and
hold it for a slow count of twelve. As you gradually
exhale, see in your mind's eye the white cloud descend
upon you and envelop your entire body. When properly
performed, you will feel a tingling sensation throughout
your body. This usually will start at the feet and the
hands and work its way inward and upward throughout
your body to finally include your head. This is the
subtle soul energy so necessary to our physical,
emotional and mental well-being.*

*Sit in quiet then for three or four minutes until the
tingling sensation wears away. Then repeat the entire
exercise. After the second repetition, rest about five
minutes and then perform it once more, again resting
afterward about five minutes. You should now be
sufficiently well charged with psychic energy to proceed
with exercise 3.*

*3. After the five-minute period of relaxation
proceed immediately to the next step as follows:*

*Remain sitting or lying as you were and once again
visualize the brilliant white cloud above your head.
When it is clear in your mind's eye, use the energy you
have just accumulated to lift yourself up into the cloud.
Do not visualize the cloud coming down to your level
but instead see yourself moving up and out of your
body to a place within the cloud above you. As you do*

this, take a deep breath and hold it for the count of twelve. Then as you slowly exhale, feel yourself slide back into your physical vehicle.

Do this again after a rest and then a third time. Perform this entire sequence once a day and after a month or two you will observe marked changes for the better taking place. In each person these first changes will vary depending upon his or her needs.

By far, the most important application for consciousness expansion is toward your own personal growth. Other advantages you can expect are expanding your self-image, creativity, resistance to stress, performance in any task, and ability to learn.

This becomes a chain reaction. Your improvement of the mind-body-spirit connection creates an unstoppable momentum that has no boundaries. In effect, the sky is the limit. Your results will have practical applications.

This is not going to mean much if you are not happy. In my Los Angeles office I see many wealthy, famous and powerful people. They have everything they want, except for one thing. They are miserable. It may be difficult to comprehend how someone in this position could be so unhappy. These celebrity patients do not request my hypnotherapy services to spend time bragging about how great their life is. Read the newspaper and follow the electronic media to substantiate what I am saying. Do you not hear about the many dysfunctional and self-defeating behaviors of the rich and famous?

Applying this to your own life, remember that your motivation and spiritual awareness are the most important qualities a person can have. The rest is simply a matter of time and application. Solving your personal problems is not just a nice thing to do. It is your duty to yourself and the universe to continually grow and lay the foundation for custom designing your own destiny.

Establish Your Karmic Purpose

This script trains you to find out what your karmic purpose is. I cannot overemphasize the importance of this information:

Now listen very carefully. I want you to imagine a bright white light coming down from above and entering the top of your head. Filling your entire body. See it, feel it and it becomes reality. Now imagine an aura of pure white light emanating from your heart region. Again surrounding your entire body. Protecting you. See it, feel it and it becomes reality. Now only your Masters and Guides and highly evolved loving entities who mean you well will be able to influence you during this or any other hypnotic session. You are totally protected by this aura of pure white light.

In a few moments I am going to count from 1 to 20. As I do so you will feel yourself rising up to the superconscious mind level where you will be able to receive information from your Masters and Guides. You will also be able to overview all of your past,

287

present and future lives. Number 1, - rising up. 2, 3, 4, - rising higher. 5, 6, 7, - letting information flow. 8, 9, 10, - you are halfway there. 11, 12, 13, - feel yourself rising even higher. 14, 15, 16, - almost there. 17, 18, 19, number 20, - you are there. Take a moment and orient yourself to the superconscious mind level.

Play New Age Music For 1 Minute

Now slowly and carefully state your desire for information or an experience and let this superconscious mind level work for you.

Your Higher Self has all the answers to the question "What is my karmic purpose?" Let your perfect component of your soul's energy assist you in learning why you chose this particular lifetime, and exactly what it is you are supposed to accomplish to complete this karmic sub-cycle. Ask your Higher Self to answer the question "What is my karmic purpose?" Do this now.

Play New Age Music For 5 Minutes

Let your superconscious mind now establish a complete and global communication and assessment of your karmic purpose. Begin with simple goals or purposes and move on to more advanced ones as you allow and encourage your Higher Self to let this information flow. You are raising your soul's frequency and vibration rate while this is occurring. Do this now:

Play New Age Music For 4 Minutes

All right now. Sleep now and rest. You did very well. Listen very carefully. I'm going to count forward now from 1 to 5. When I reach the count of 5 you will be back in the present, you will be able to remember everything you experienced and re-experienced, you'll feel very relaxed refreshed, you'll be able to do whatever you have planned for the rest of the day or evening. You'll feel very positive about what you've just experienced and very motivated about your confidence and ability to play this tape again to experience the superconscious mind level. All right now. 1,   - very, very deep; 2, - you're getting a little bit lighter; 3,   - you're getting much, much lighter; 4, - very, very light. 5,   - awaken. Wide awake, and refreshed.

How To Specifically Attain Psychic Empowerment

The first question you need to ask yourself is, "How do I define power?" Some people feel power by controlling the behavior of others, such as children, spouses, employees, etc. This is a form of having power over someone and has no spiritual basis whatsoever. It is merely a sign of insecurity.

Another way of experiencing power is by being in a certain frame of mind. Examples of this are using humor to deal with stress, being understanding or patient and being in touch with and expressing your feelings. By experiencing power as a result of your ability to both receive the energy of others and appropriately respond to it, you are demonstrating a more spiritual basis to your behavior.

Third, you may well experience power by assisting others to learn, grow and become independent. This is a true form of empowerment, and is a vital component of taking charge of your life. A balance of the last two forms of power establishes a healthy order and enables us to respond to the universe's challenges so that we may grow spiritually.

A second factor in psychic empowerment is represented by our unwillingness to be distracted from our vision during the trials and tribulations of life. This is commitment, and it results in confidence, fulfillment, and pride in our achievements. The key to establishing commitment is having a vision that both excites and motivates us. The use of affirmations, visualizations and superconscious mind taps enables us to create a vision that we can believe in.

Discipline is required to dedicate a certain part of our day to our vision. The more compelling our vision, the easier it is to establish and maintain this vision. We always need to keep abreast of why we are doing what we are engaged in. Commitment results from a compelling vision, and this results in discipline. Any distractions or indiscretions in our discipline can be quickly resolved by reaffirming our vision.

When I use the term Higher Self, I am specifically referring to the perfect component of our soul's energy that relates information to our conscious mind in the form of intuition, hunches and visions.

Using the superconscious mind technique involves quieting your mind and turning off the mental chatter of your rational mind. Next, you can ask your Higher Self for any information you desire. You must develop trust in this perfect component of your soul's energy. Last, you need to act upon these instructions for putting your game plan into action to realize abundance and spiritual growth.

Love is always a component of psychic empowerment. To love ourselves, to love another, and to be loved by another, all stimulate us to expand and open. It is in this state of loving openness that we are most capable of profound growth. Love is the most powerful motivating force in the universe. There can be no spiritual growth if love is conditional, or if you approach your goals from a perspective of pain, fear, "shoulds" or other obligations.

Self-love is the most important relationship we have. By validating, nurturing and accepting ourselves unconditionally, we eliminate any tendency to become codependent. This inner love is quite different from the external love that most of us consider in our definition of this term.

The superconscious mind tap and other examples of hypnosis, meditation and so on commit us to self-exploration. Love is now cultivated as you open to deeper parts of yourself, the more in touch with your true nature you get and the more you discover its essence - love. The compassion and patience we have for others and the ability to overcome fears and negativity are represented by our inner love.

Truth is another component of psychic empowerment. When we find our ultimate truth and live our lives based on this truth, psychic empowerment naturally results.

Here is a simple exercise to assist you in removing past hurts. Precede this with playing your superconscious mind tape:

1.   Visualize yourself on a long, isolated highway. This road has healing qualities at each fork in this expansive road. You may travel either back or forward in time on this road by simply using the drive or reverse gear on your car.

2.   Using the reverse gear, back up on this road to a time when you experienced a traumatic hurt in your life. Come to a healing fork in this road and communicate with the person responsible for this hurt. It may very well have been yourself at a young age who generated this self-hurt. Carry on a conversation with this individual (or yourself) and express why you were hurt.

3.   Listen to this other person and resolve that hurt now in this healing fork in the road. Pay strict attention to the person's truth while immersing yourself in the healing energy at this fork in the road. Feel yourself being healed and empowered.

4. *Now place your car in the drive gear and move forward in time beyond the present to five years in the future. Arrive at a healing fork in the road and note how this hurt is long gone. See how your life has changed as a result of this cleansing, and again immerse yourself in the healing energy of this fork in the road.*

Chapter 15
Case Histories

Cal

Cal contacted my office in 1983 with regard to changing his life. He needed "major surgery," as he stated, on the path his life had taken. This 39-year-old university professor was simply frustrated with his life.

He had moved from city to city assuming various positions with different universities, but just wasn't going anywhere professionally. More important, he hated teaching. His fields were accounting and real estate, and he wanted to be a financially independent entrepreneur. His goal was to become an active real estate investor in up-scale commercial properties. He had no previous practical experience in this area, although was well qualified academically.

Cal was married and had two teenage children. There were no significant family problems with his wife and children. Cal just wanted to move on with his life and didn't know how to empower himself. He had read the original version of my first book, *Past Lives——Future Lives*, and this piqued his interest about undergoing some age progressions.

Skepticism was most definitely a component of Cal's personality. He did not share a metaphysical belief system, but one section of *Past Lives——Future Lives* motivated him to contact my office. That section described a television newscaster who went into the future by a week to ten days and documented his description of news events before they happened.

Another episode that preceded Cal's purchasing my first book occurred the previous year. He heard me one evening when I hosted a radio show called "Insights into Parapsychology." One of the callers that fateful evening was a former patient of mine who described how he used my age progression tape to win $5,000 in the state lottery following his therapy.

I worked with Cal for two months. During this time the super-conscious mind tap was used to train him to raise his energy to rise above his former vulnerability to such issues as:

- Indecisiveness. He was one of the most indecisive and insecure patient whom I treated during the 1980s.

- Procrastination.
- Lip biting.
- Smoking.
- Headaches.
- Insomnia.

Cal made excellent progress and was ready for his age progressions as I described in chapter 12. His five frequencies were quite typical in that one was average, one was below average and the third very depressing. That left frequencies 4 and 5 as quite attractive.

The only problem Cal had was deciding between frequencies 4 and 5. It wasn't that Cal was still indecisive in general; it was that the content of these frequencies departed from the usual pattern. Frequency number 4 was fairly good for the next five years, and in 1988 it was fantastic. Cal perceived himself as living in the Caribbean, owning a yacht and being totally fulfilled in his life.

Frequency number 5 was much better than number 4 during the 1983 to 1988 time frame, but after 1988 was not as desirable as number 4. Cal's dilemma was which to choose. Does he go for immediate gratification and select frequency 5, or is he patient and oriented toward number 4?

To illustrate just how empowered Cal became (this even surprised me!) he asked me to program him for frequency 5 now, and in 1988 he wanted to return to my office and have me reprogram him for number 4.

You will recall Cal's initial request was for major surgery - psychic surgery, that is. I had never done that before, and being an open-minded scientist and clinician, I accepted the metaphysical gauntlet laid at my hypnotherapeutic feet.

I informed Cal that it was his responsibility to contact me in five years. What he didn't know was that I placed his name in a special file and made a note to call him in 1988.

In late December of 1987 Cal called me. He had quit his teaching position and was very happy. Cal's frequency number 5 had manifested as he had visualized it nearly five years before. It took only one session to reprogram him to frequency number 4. That was the last I ever saw of Cal. I did ask him to keep me posted on his progress, since this was an experiment in quantum physics.

Although I never saw Cal again, I most certainly heard from him. One hot summer Sunday afternoon in 1994, I received a call on my portable phone while swimming in my pool and observing my two miniature schnauzers, Phoenix and Alpha, playing. Cal was calling from a portable phone, on his yacht no less, to update me on his life. Yes, everything he perceived had come to pass. He lived in the Caribbean and was a very wealthy and fulfilled real estate investor, among other enterprises. His children were established in their own professional lives, and he and his wife were just plain happy. They both invited me to be a guest at their mansion. Cal expressed his undying gratitude for my help. I don't think he heard me when I reinforced the concept that I had very little to do with his success. Cal did 98 percent of the work in his REM cycle and custom designed his own destiny.

Valerie

Valerie's case offers so many examples of empowerment and custom designing her own destiny that this brief summary cannot possibly do her justice. This example also offers medical documentation to disprove the "wishful thinking" argument.

Valerie called my Los Angeles office in June of 1993 in a dire panic. She had received a "vision" during a dream that clearly stated that her mother, Joann, was going to die by December 19 (Joann's birthday) that year.

Valerie was a conventional woman from a conservative background. She had no previous history of precognitive dreams, and this was like no other dream this 30-year-old housewife and mother had ever experienced.

Joann was more than just Valerie's mother; she was her best friend. A loss such as this would be devastating to Valerie. I am the last person she would be expected to call, considering her conservative background and dislike of anything metaphysical.

I can still remember that initial telephone call. "I don't want any regressions or progressions, Dr. Goldberg, just help me to deal with my mother's impending death!"

Joann had seen her regular physician just a few months before and received a clean bill of health. Valerie's husband, Scott, dismissed his wife's dream as just that, a bad dream. Scott was also rather conservative, and neither he nor his wife had previous experiences or interest in paranormal phenomena.

Valerie had other goals that we worked on. She was a housewife, but longed to become involved in real estate sales. Scott was a very successful real estate salesman, and he functioned as a model for Valerie.

After conducting a series of superconscious mind taps, some unusual things began happening in Valerie's current frequency. Scott received a rather large raise just three weeks after her initial session. Valerie's relationship with her mother-in-law, Judy, improved dramatically. Judy had always shown intense dislike for Valerie, but this transformed into love and understanding.

Valerie's vision and the "New-You" technique revealed that Joann had a medical problem that would end her life. Valerie was programmed to select the frequency in which her mother would be alive, and in which Valerie would lose weight.

Joann was not particularly interested in making another appointment with her physician. Valerie cajoled her mother into finally consenting to seeing the latter's doctor one more time. As a result of this second exam, Joann was informed that she had a three-centimeter kidney stone and surgery was scheduled. This was not an easy procedure, but Joann did fine. Her physician told her that she most likely would have died if that kidney stone hadn't been removed. In addition, he noted that her high blood pressure, which had been medically monitored for years, was now dangerously out of control. He corrected that by increasing the dosage of her medication.

Valerie saved Joann's life and her reward manifested itself in other ways. Her marriage improved, she lost weight and began taking better care of herself in general.

Another talent manifested itself as Valerie's intuition began to grow. Naturally, I would explain this as her becoming expert at accessing her Higher Self and viewing her future frequency. She developed a psychic bond with both Judy and Joann.

On one occasion Valerie had a shockingly accurate progression. She and Scott decided to move to Woodland Hills and were looking at their new home in January of 1994. Valerie went into a trance and saw destruction all around this home. They moved in anyway and exactly two weeks later the Northridge earthquake hit and her new home suffered serious damage.

Valerie and her family had to leave their new home for over three weeks. All turned out well and they moved back in. I remember her asking me why my home, also in Woodland Hills, had received so little damage. I replied, "I guess I just have good karma."

By the end of 1994, Valerie was hired as a real estate secretary and soon began selling properties herself. She is today a successful real estate saleswoman.

One other aspect of Valerie's case is worth mentioning. When I first worked with Valerie she had a low self-image. She had found out quite a bit about me from reading my first book, *Past Lives——Future_Lives*, and hearing about my various interviews on television and radio. I recall a comment she made at the time. "I could never do an interview. Not only would I be so nervous, but who would want to hear about my boring life?"

Empowerment is one of the most important benefits of the "New-You" technique. Valerie did do television interviews with me, in fact, quite a few of them. You may have seen her on the *Jerry Springer Show*, which aired on January 7, 1994 and during which Scott and Judy accompanied her.

The ironic thing about the Jerry Springer interview was that we were all in Chicago on Sunday, December 19, 1993, having dinner at Oprah Winfrey's restaurant the night before the taping. This was Joannn's birthday and the day she would have died if Valerie's Higher Self had not intervened.

Valerie also was on CNBC with me on Geraldo Rivera's new show; the CBS 11:00 P.M. News following the airing of my television movie, *Search for Grace* (based on my book titled *The Search for Grace*); Fox's *Encounters*; and NBC's *The Other Side*. Not bad for a woman who thought nobody cared about her "boring life."

Valerie summed up her experiences by stating:

> "This supreme energy showed me the importance and uniqueness of my spirit - of everyone's spirit. Each person's existence played an integral part of the workings of the universe. I had a special role, a unique role that only I could fill. I was bathed in feelings of worth, value and complete love. Instinctively, I knew that I had just been cradled in the arms of the divine."

On June 24, 1996, I received the following letter from Valerie:
    "Dear Dr. Goldberg,

    I wanted to take this opportunity to thank you for all the information and guidance you've given me along the way.

    I feel I have come so far - emotionally, spiritually and in general since I made the smart decision of using your hypnosis methods for self-improvement.

    You are not only a brilliant hypnotherapist, but also a very kind and generous person. I consider you our family friend.

    Not many people would give their time, information and inspiration as freely as you do.

    Words can't thank you enough! I hope to see you and hear from you soon.

                    Sincerely,

                    Valerie"

Mary

Mary's case represents another medically documented example of age progression and the "New-You" technique. Mary came to my Los Angeles office in July of 1993 with a very serious problem. She had AIDS. Her T4 lymphocyte count was around 50, which is not very good. Anything below 200 with an HIV positive status is an active case of AIDS.

Mary was depressed and felt there was no hope for her. She had seen me on Tom Snyder's CNBC show and immediately obtained a copy of my first book, *Past Lives——Future Lives*. She was now retired from teaching with a disability (AIDS).

Writing was an interest of hers, and she wanted to pursue it successfully now that she had the time to devote to it.

I guided her through the superconscious mind tap technique and proceeded with her age progressions. The frequencies she described were most depressing. In all but one she died rather young, these were lonely and frustrating frequencies.

The ideal frequency she chose surprised even me. On this path she lived a relatively long life and in the very near future was to be removed from an experimental AIDS vaccine and yet heal her body by herself. That is not what most patients with terminal illnesses describe. Her writing career was to be successful with articles and books to her credit.

As it turned out, Mary was placed on an experimental vaccine, Nevirapine, and was later informed that it was ineffective. She was taken off this drug and within 10 weeks her T4 count rose from 50 to 150!

The following year, she had an article published in a major magazine and she felt great. She later informed me she had completed a manuscript for a novel and was actively seeking an agent. In 1997, I received a postcard from her with the cover of her novel, now in its second edition from a major publisher.

All in all Mary successfully used the "New-You" Technique to help herself with the most serious disease known to mankind. Her case gives hope to all and demonstrates the unlimited power of the subconscious.

Sheila

Sheila called my office after reading a scientific article of mine in 1990 titled, "The clinical use of hypnotic regression and progression in hypnotherapy." Actually, her father, a psychologist in Europe, read this article initially and recommended it to her.

When Sheila called me from Europe I detected a tremendous amount of anxiety in her voice. She was in her last year of college and a psychology major. Her main issue dealt with a complete lack of empowerment and high levels of anxiety about her future.

She was her parents' only child and most definitely was "daddy's little girl." These were her words, and she wanted to "do her own thing," and she just wasn't sure that psychology was it. Her grades in school weren't bad, but there was no heart and soul in her attitude toward the profession that her father most definitely urged her to pursue.

Sheila was frustrated and burned out with the talk therapy approaches to her future career. This just added to her anxieties. She found my article fascinating and subsequently read my book, *Past Lives——Future Lives*.

In the summer of 1990 Sheila came to my office for five days of intensive hypnotherapy. Throughout her week in Los Angeles, she was trained in the superconscious mind tap, age progression and the "New-You" Technique. She had many questions about my work and expressed great interest and excitement in practicing this sub-specialty herself.

I explained to her that I train many therapists and before she returned home she purchased my Metaphysical Training Program cassette album, videotape and training manual. These aids orient therapists in the use of these techniques in their own practices. Even non-therapists can work with these training vehicles to maximize the effect of their work with me. Many of those that have purchased this kit have never seen me and merely use these aids for their own self-empowerment.

Throughout Sheila's one-week stay in Los Angeles, we dealt with her self-image, issues related to her father, anxiety, and a myriad of other self-defeating sequences. The ideal frequency she selected showed her "New-You" persona to be a practicing psychologist in her home country using many of my techniques.

This ideal path presented her as being married to a physician, having a hypnotherapy-based psychotherapy practice and a fulfilled and empowered life on many levels. When she left my office, Sheila was beaming with energy and couldn't wait to return to school for her last year as an undergraduate.

In the spring of 1996 I received a call from another young woman from Sheila's home country. She was referred by Sheila for the "New-You" technique. I naturally inquired about my former patient, and this new patient (Darla) stated that she would have Sheila get in touch with me.

Sheila did call me about two weeks later to update me on her "New-You" life. She had gone on to receive a doctorate in psychology and had set up a practice specializing in hypnotherapy. Yes, she is using a modified form of the "New-You" approach in her practice.

My former patient also informed me that she had married a physician and is happier than she could have possibly imagined. Her issues with her father were also resolved, since she no longer felt obligated to please him. He is quite proud of his "little girl," and is more open to the "unusual" approach she applies in her practice.

This type of case is most rewarding to me as a professional. I find it very fulfilling to train my colleagues, even a "budding" professional. Sheila not only "got her act together," but she can now apply this form of empowerment and custom designing of destinies to countless thousands of her patients well into the twenty-first century.

Nicki

Nicki's case is quite typical of the requests for my services among working women. She was a 36-year-old regional manager for a large East Coast company and presented herself with a large number of issues. These were:

- Insomnia
- Sexual dysfunction
- Overeating
- Excessive use of alcohol
- Poor relationships with her three children
- Fear of flying
- Depression

Of all of these issues, Nicki pointed to the fear of flying as being her top priority. She had to fly regularly as part of her job responsibilities. I informed her that all her issues were psychosomatic, and we would deal with each of them.

I should point out at this time that Nicki had been to a gynecologist and internist to have a series of tests administered. There were no organic (medical) bases for any of her complaints.

At first Nicki was skeptical and unsure of her ability to empower herself. She had tried many forms of therapy and NEW AGE approaches prior to coming to my office in the spring of 1991. Nicki's fears centered around the two major theoretical paradigms she had been exposed to. One form, related to conventional therapy, amounted to a type of therapeutic reductionism: "People hurt me because their parents, family, etc., hurt them. All I can do is keep the pain to a minimum and try my best to prevent it from being passed on."

Another point of view was her interpretation of the "New Age" theme, which was: "My own Higher Self selected and designed this series of hurts and problems so I could work through my karma."

My empowerment and "New-You" Technique had never crossed her mind before. It was a completely foreign approach, and she just felt it was "too good to be true." However, she was open to this method and had to do something to get her life on a more fulfilling path. At the young age of thirty-six, she didn't even want to imagine what her life would be like in five or ten years if things didn't change.

After training Nicki in the superconscious mind tap technique (cleansing), we began with the progressions. At first she was blocking the process, but I am a patient man and my methods finally took hold. Nicki's five frequencies were actually quite typical, and she selected her ideal path without hesitation.

This ideal frequency showed that Nicki was to remove her fear of flying, insomnia, alcohol abuse and develop better eating habits by the end of 1991. Before 1992 came to a close, she would resolve her sexual dysfunction issues (frigidity), depression, and develop a more functional relationship with her children and husband.

The next time I heard from Nicki was in July of 1994. She had seen my CBS movie, *Search for Grace*, and called to tell me how much she enjoyed both the movie and book.

I asked her for an update and she informed me that each of her goals was accomplished according to the schedule she related in her selected ideal frequency.

The only exception was that her frigidity was resolved in 1991, not in the following year as her frequency indicated. She didn't complain about that circumstance and thanked me for introducing her to her "New-You". It is I who owe you my appreciation and gratitude, Nicki, for illustrating that anyone can "be all they can be" through the application of simple and natural methods.

Conclusion

My purpose in writing this book is to demonstrate the power of mind over matter. More specifically, I am attempting to illustrate the enormous potential we all have to use our mind to empower ourselves and custom design our own destiny.

As a scientist and clinician, I naturally draw upon the hard sciences of quantum mechanics (the new physics) and psychoneuro-immunology (PNI) to support my paradigms. For example, a recent New Zealand study illustrates just how powerful the mind is in altering our behavior.

Ninety patients faced with life-threatening illnesses (heart attacks and breast cancer) reported the following positive changes in their lives after these crises:

- 51% reported healthy lifestyle changes.
- 28% reported an increase in their appreciation of life and health.

- 21% noted improved relationships with loved ones.

Improved empathy toward others, feeling fortunate in having been given a second chance and a shift in personal priorities was also noted.[1] Fortunately, you do not have to wait for a life-threatening illness to empower yourself and place yourself in a position to custom design your own destiny. Simply following the recommendations and exercises in this book will assist you in achieving any goal you desire.

In another study, men who either expressed their anger outwardly in a violent manner (aggressive style) or those who held in their anger (passive style) had significantly higher total cholesterol and LDL (bad cholesterol) levels as compared to men who dealt with anger in a more assertive manner.[2]

We are engineered as goal-seeking mechanisms. When we have no personal goal that interests and "means something" to us, we are apt to "go around in circles," feel "lost" and find life itself "aimless," and "purposeless." We are built to conquer environment, solve problems, attain goals, and we find no real satisfaction or happiness in life

---

[1] K.J. Buick and Dr. Weinman, "Positive effects of illness reported by myocardial infarction, and breast cancer patients" (Abstract). *Psychosomatic Medicine* 58 (1996):76.

[2] T.O. Engelbretson and C.M. Stoney, "Anger expression and lipid concentrations. *International Journal of Behavioral Medicine* 2(4) (1995): 281-298.

without obstacles to conquer and goals to achieve. People who say that life is not worthwhile are really saying that they themselves have no personal goals that are worthwhile.

Always have something ahead of you to look forward to - to work for and hope for. Look forward, not backward. Develop what one of the automobile manufacturers calls "the forward look." Develop "nostalgia for the future" instead of for the past. The "forward look" and a "nostalgia for the future" can keep you youthful. Even your body doesn't function well when you stop being a goal striver and have nothing to look forward to. This is the reason why very often when a man retires, he dies shortly thereafter. When you are not goal striving, not looking forward, you're not really living.

The vibrations of fear pass from one mind to another just as quickly and as surely as the sound of the human voice passes from the broadcasting station to the receiving set of a radio. The person who gives expression by word of mouth to negative or destructive thoughts is practically certain to experience the results of those words in the form of a destructive kickback.

These thought impulses are not only damaging to others, but they also imbed themselves in the subconscious mind of the person releasing them, and there become a part of his character. To be successful, you must find peace of mind, acquire the material needs of life, and above all, attain happiness. All these evidences of success begin in the form of thought impulses.

You may control your own mind; you have the power to feed it whatever thought impulses you choose. With this privilege goes the responsibility of using it constructively. You truly are the master of your destiny, just as you control your own thoughts. You have the power to influence, direct and eventually control your own environment.

Don't wait to achieve goals. If you want to enjoy a richer life, begin each day by improving yourself, empowering your soul and custom designing your own destiny. Life is what you are looking for. If you are searching for everything that's wrong with people and the world, that's what you'll find. You will then prove to yourself that the world and its people are no good. But if you look for the gold in those around you, your life will be rich with friends.

Since science fails to address our inner world of beliefs, thoughts and emotions in their cause-and-effect paradigms, all metaphysical and spiritual principles are ignored. The role of consciousness in creating our reality daily is only dealt with by quantum physics, and most conventional scientists scoff at that discipline. Scientists mostly brush aside all theories involving the holistic integration of body, mind and soul.

Spirituality is derived from the word spirit, which *The American Heritage Dictionary* defines as "the vital principle or animating force traditionally believed to be within living beings." How can we become psychically empowered (or repowered) unless we possess this vital principle or animating force within our being? The answer is simple; we can't.

If we truly want to have more control over our future, we must change the way we think about ourselves and the universe. Altering our beliefs through subconscious reprogramming and super-conscious mind taps represents the first step toward leading a fuller and more satisfying life. This book has attempted to detail specific ways to accomplish these goals and allow you to empower yourself.

In addition to acquiring a more meaningful and productive life, you will experience benefits as you follow this system to its natural conclusion. These additional benefits include:

> Increased activity.
> Good fortune in all aspects of your life.
> Better relationships with greater honest and openness.
> Reduced stress.
> Improved health and resistance to disease, both physical and mental.
> The attainment of abundance.
> Spiritual growth, accompanied by feelings of peace, inner joy and love.

As you allow this process of spiritual unfoldment to take place, life becomes more meaningful. The full beauty of the universe and all its wonders are revealed as you learn to release your fears and embrace unconditional love. The rate of your enlightenment depends upon your level of commitment and willingness to face your fears. Only your "heart-of-heart" efforts can accomplish the goal of custom designing your own destiny.

Realistic Idealism

My definition of success has a great deal to do with high ideals and what is practically possible. That is why I refer to it as realistic idealism. This description has nothing to do with prestige or any other superficial concept.

Creative accomplishment and total fulfillment are major components of realistic idealism. Do not attempt to be a success; rather, be successful. To attempt to be a success by other people's superficial criteria will usually result in frustration, neurotic behavior and unhappiness.

You will create your own brand of happiness and fulfillment by creatively striving for goals, goals that are a product of your needs, talents, aspirations and soul's purpose.

I have presented several simple techniques to train you to empower yourself, visualize goals and bring your successful future into your current awareness. Use these methods well and feel free to contact me to share your joy of custom designing your own destiny.

Bibliography

Adams, J. D. *Understanding and Managing Stress*. San Diego: University Associates, 1980.

Argyle, M. *The Psychology of Interpersonal Behavior*. Baltimore: Pelican Publications, 1967.

Banquet, J. P. "Spectral analysis of the EEG in meditation." *Electroencephalography and Clinical Neurophysiology*. 1973: *35*, 143-151.

Bateson, M. *Composing a Life*. New York: Plume, 1989.

Benson, H. *The Relaxation Response*. Boston: G. K. Hall, 1976.

Bronowski, J. *The Origins of Knowledge and Imagination*. New Haven: Yale University Press, 1978.

Buick, K. J. and Weinman, D. "Positive effects of illness reported by myocardial infarction and breast cancer patients." *Psychosomatic Medicine*, 1996: *58*, 76.

Burns, D. *Feeling Good*. New York: William Morrow & Company, 1980.

Carrington, P. *Freedom in Meditation*. New York: Doubleday, 1977.

Chapman, A. H. *Put Offs and Come Ons*. New York: Putnam, 1968.

Cotler, S. and Guerra, J. *Assertion Training: A Humanistic-Behavioral Guide to Dignity*. Englewood Cliffs, N.J.: Prentice-Hall, 1976.

Da Free J. *The Enlightenment of the Whole Body*. San Rafael, CA: Dawn Horse Press, 1980.

D'Espagnat, B. "Quantum Theory and Reality." *Scientific American*, 1979: *241*, 158-160.

Dunne, J. W. *An Experiment with Time*. New York: Macmillan, 1927.

Engelbretson, T. O. and Stoney, C. M. "Anger expression and lipid concentrations." *International Journal of Behavioral Medicine*, 1995: *2*(4), 281-298.

Fast, J. *Body Language*. Philadelphia: M. Evans and Co. Inc., 1970.

Fritz, R. *Nobody Gets Rich Working for Somebody Else*. Menlo Park, CA: Crisp Pub., 1993.

Goldberg, B. *Soul Healing*. St. Paul: Llewellyn Pub. 1996.
_____. *The Search for Grace: The True Story of Murder and Reincarnation*. St. Paul: Llewellyn Pub., 1997.
_____. *New Age Hypnosis*. St. Paul: Llewellyn Pub. 1998.
_____. *Astral Voyages: Mastering the Art of Soul Travel*. St. Paul: Llewellyn, 1999.
_____. *Look Younger, Live Longer: Add 25 to 50 Quality Years to Your Life, Naturally*. St. Paul: Llewellyn Pub. 1998.
_____. *Past Lives——Future Lives*. New York: Ballantine Books, 1988.
_____. "Slowing down the aging process through the use of altered states of consciousness: A review of the medical literature." *Psychology—A Journal of Human Behavior*, 1995: *32*(2), 19-22.
_____. "Regression and Progression in Past Life Therapy." *National Guild of Hypnotists Newsletter*, 1994: Jan/Feb,1, 10.
_____. "Quantum Physics and its application to past life regression and future life progression hypnotherapy." *Journal of Regression Therapy*, 1993: 7(1), 89-93.

Bibliography

_____, "Depression: a past life cause." *National Guild of Hypnotists Newsletter*, 1993: Oct/Nov, 7, 14.

_____, "The clinical use of hypnotic regression and progression in hypnotherapy." *Psychology——A Journal of Human Behavior*, 1990: *27*(1), 43-48.

_____, "The treatment of cancer through hypnosis." *Psychology——A Journal of Human Behavior*, 1985: *3*(4), 36-39.

_____, "Hypnosis and the immune response." *International Journal of Psychosomatics*, 1985: *32*(3), 34-36.

_____. "Treating dental phobias through past life therapy: a case report." *Journal of the Maryland State Dental Association*, 1984: *27*(3), 137-139.

Green, E., and Green A. *Beyond Biofeedback*. New York: Delacorte Press, 1989.

Gula, R. *Nonsense: How to Overcome It*. New York: Stein & Day, 1979.

Gunn, J. A. *The Problem of Time*. London: Allen & Unwin, 1929.

Hilgrad, E. "Altered States of Awareness." *Journal of Nervous and Mental Disease*, 1969: *149*, 68-79.

Hoeing, J. Medical Research on Yoga. 1968, *2*, 69-89. *Confinia Psychiatrica*.

Honorton, C. Relationship between EEG Alpha activity and ESP card guessing performance. *Journal of the American Society for Psychical Research*, 1969: *63*, 365-374.

Hoover, L. E. "Alpha and the First Step to a New Level of Reality." *Human Behavior*, 1972: May-June, *3*.

Hume, D. *An Enquiry Concerning Human Understanding*, edited by P. H. Nidditch. New York: The Liberal Arts Press, 1975.

Israeli, N. "Some Aspects of the Social Psychology of Futurism." *Journal of Abnormal Social Psychology*, 1930: *25*, 121-132.

_____. "Group predictions of future events." *Journal of Social Psychology*, 1933: 4, 201-222.

Kamiya, J. "A Fourth Dimension of Consciousness." *Journal of Experimental Medicine and Surgery*, 1969, *27*, 13-18.

Karagulla, S. *Breakthrough to Creativity*. Santa Monica, CA: De-Vross and Co., 1967.

Krippner, S., and Hughes, W. "Dreams and Human Potential." *Journal of Humanistic Psychology*. Spring, 1970, *10*, (1), 1-19.

Krippner, S. and Ullman, M. "Telepathy and Dreams: A Controlled Experiment With Electroencephalogram, Electro-Oculogram Monitoring." *Journal of Nervous and Mental Disease*, 1970: 151, 394-402.

Kushner, H. S. *When All You've Ever Wanted Isn't Enough*. New York: Summit Books, 1986.

Lecky, Prescott. *Self-Consistency: A Theory of Personality*. New York: Shoe String Press, 1961.

Lewis, H. *A Question of Values, Six Ways We Make the Personal Choices That Shape Our Lives*. San Francisco: Harper & Row, 1990.

Llinas, R. (ed). *The Workings of the Brain*. New York: Freeman & Co., 1990.

London, P., Hart, J., and Leivovitz, M. "EEG Alpha Rhythms and Susceptibility to Hypnosis." *Nature*, 1968, *219*, 71-72.

Luce, G. *Body Time*. New York: Pantheon, 1971.

Bibliography

Luthe, W. *Autogenic Therapy, Research and Theory*. New York and London: Grune and Stratton, 1970.

Lynch, J., Orne, M., Paskewitz, D., and Costello. J. "An Analysis of the Feedback Control of Alpha Activity." *Conditional Reflex*, 1970: *5*, 185-86.

Lynch, J., and Paskewitz, D. "On the Mechanisms of the Feedback Control of Human Brain Wave Activity." *Journal of Nervous and Mental Disease*, 1971: *153*, 205-17.

Maxwell, M. and Verena, T. *Seeing the Invisible*. London: Arkana, 1990.

Mihalasky, J., and Dean, D. *PSI Research*. Newark, N.J.: Newark College of Engineering, 1971.

Morrell, E. *The 25th Man*. Montclair, N.J.: New Era Pub. Co., 1924.

Mulholland, T. "The Concept of Attention and the Electroencephalographic Alpha Rhythms," in C. Evans and T. Mulholland (eds.), *Attention in Neurophysiology*. London: Butterworths, 1969.

Nierenberg, G. *The Art of Negotiating*. New York: Hawthorn Books, Inc., 1968.

Nierenberg, G. and Calero, H. *How To Read A Person Like A Book*. New York: Simon & Schuster, 1971.

Norman, Richard. *The Moral Philosophers: An Introduction to Ethics*. New York: Oxford University Press, 1983.

Ornstein, R., and Thompson, R.F. *The Amazing Brain*. Boston: Houghton Mifflin, 1984.

Ornstein, R. and Sobel, D. *The Healing Brain*. New York: Simon & Schuster, 1988.

Rusell, P. *The White Hole in Time*. New York: Harper Collins, 1992.

Scheflen, A. E. *Body Language and the Social Order*. Englewood Cliffs, N.J.: Prentice Hall, 1972.

Sinetar, M. *Do What You Love, The Money Will Follow*. New York: Dell, 1989.
_____. New York: St. Martin's Griffin, *To Build The Life You Want, Create the Work You Love* 1995.

Storr, A. *Human Aggression*. New York: Bantam Books, 1970.

Talbot, M. *The Holographic Universe*. New York: Harper Collins, 1991.

Tart, C. *Altered States of Consciousness*. New York: John Wiley & Sons, 1969.
_____. *Open Mind, Discriminating Mind*. New York, Harper Collins, 1989.

Vaillant, G. *Adaptation to Life*. Boston: Little, Brown & Co., 1977.

Wheat, E. *Secret Choices: Personal Decisions That Affect Your Marriage*. Grand Rapids, MI: Zonderman, 1989.

Wolf, F. A. *Taking the Quantum Leap*. New York: Harper & Row, 1981.

Bibliography

_____. *Parallel Universes: The Search for Other Worlds*. New York: Simon and Schuster, 1988.

Wolf, F.A. and Toben B. *Space-Time and Beyond*. New York: Bantam Books, 1982.

Wolman, B., and Ullman, M. *Handbook of States of Consciosness*. New York: Van Nostrand Rheinhold, 1986.

Other Books by Dr. Bruce Goldberg
Past Lives—Future Lives
Soul Healing
*The Search for Grace: A Documented
    Case of Murder and Reincarnation*
*Peaceful Transition: The Art of
    Conscious Dying and the
    Liberation of the Soul*
New Age Hypnosis
*Karmic Capitalism: A Spiritual
    Approach to Financial
    Independence*
Unleash Your Psychic Powers
*Look Younger and Live Longer: Add
    25 to 50 Quality Years to Your
    Life Naturally*
*Protected by the Light: The Complete
    Book of Psychic Self Defense*
*Time Travelers from Our Future: A
    Fifth Dimension Odyssey*
*Astral Voyages: Mastering the art of
    Interdimensional Travel*
*Lose Weight Permanently and
    Naturally*
*Self-Hypnosis: Easy Ways to Hypnotize
    Your Problems Away*
*Dream Your Problems Away: Heal
    Yourself While You Sleep*
Past Lives, Future Lives Revealed

About the Author

Dr. Bruce Goldberg holds a B.A. degree in Biology and Chemistry, is a Doctor of Dental Surgery, and has an M.S. degree in Counseling Psychology. He retired from dentistry in 1989, and has concentrated on his hypnotherapy practice in Los Angeles. Dr. Goldberg was trained by the American Society of Clinical Hypnosis in the techniques and clinical applications of hypnosis in 1975.

Dr. Goldberg has interviewed on the Donahue, *Oprah, Leeza, Joan Rivers, Regis, ABC Radio, Art Bell, Tom Snyder, Jerry Springer, Jenny Jones,* and *Montel Williams* shows; by *CNN, CBS News, NBC,* and many others.

Through lectures, television and radio appearances, and newsp*aper articles, including interviews in Time* the *Los Angeles Times, USA Today,* and the *Washington Post,* he has conducted more than 35,000 past-life regressions and future-life progressions since 1974, helping thousands of patients empower themselves through these techniques. His CDs, cassette tapes and DVDs teach people self-hypnosis, and guide them into past and future lives and time travel. He gives lectures and seminars on hypnosis, regression and progression therapy, time travel, and conscious dying; he is also a consultant to corporations, attorneys, and the local and network media. His first edition of *The Search for Grace,* was made into a television movie by CBS. His third book, the award winning *Soul Healing,* is a classic on alternative medicine and psychic empowerment. *Past Lives—Future Lives* is Dr.

Goldberg's international bestseller and is the first book written on future lives (progression hypnotherapy).

Dr. Goldberg distributes CDs, cassette tapes, and DVDs to teach people self-hypnosis and to guide them into past and future lives and time travel. For information on self-hypnosis tapes, speaking engagements, or private sessions, Dr. Goldberg can be contacted directly by writing to:

Bruce Goldberg, D.D.S., M.S.
4300 Natoma Avenue, Woodland Hills, CA 91364
Telephone: (800) Karma-4-U or (800) 527-6248
Fax: (818) 704-9189
email: drbg@sbcglobal.net
Website: www.drbrucegoldberg.com

Please include a self-addressed, stamped envelope with your letter.

CPSIA information can be obtained
at www.ICGtesting.com
Printed in the USA
BVHW03s1133150518
516303BV00012B/179/P

9 781579 680145